All meaningful thought is for the sake of action, and all meaningful action is for the sake of friendship.

John Macmurray

The Personal World

John Macmurray
on self and society

Selected and introduced
by Philip Conford

Floris Books

First published in 1996 by Floris Books.

This selection © Philip Conford 1996
The copyrights listed under the acknowledgments
form a part of the copyright of this volume.
All rights reserved. No part of this publication may
be reproduced without the prior permission of
Floris Books, 15 Harrison Gardens, Edinburgh.

British Library CIP data

ISBN 0-86315-236-8

Printed in Great Britain
by Biddles Ltd, Guildford

Contents

Foreword by the Rt. Hon. Tony Blair MP   9

Acknowledgments   11

Introduction by Philip Conford   13

Editor's note   29

Abbreviations   30

1 Autobiographical   31

From Search for Reality in Religion: *John Macmurray's childhood, university studies, war experiences and the conference on the meaning of Christianity.*

2 The task of philosophy   42

Macmurray's conception of the task of philosophy; inadequacy of Descartes' Cogito; the problem facing modern philosophy.

3 The personal   54

The crisis of the personal. Analysis of the 'unity-patterns': inadequacy of the mechanical and organic in their application to human beings; the need for a pattern to do justice to the personal. The unity of living things.

4 Reason   68

The nature of reason, and how it differentiates human life.

5 The self   71

The nature of the self, which does not exist in isolation.

6 Action and habit   73

The nature of action, and the role of habit in human action. The idea of repetition as fundamental to our idea of laws of nature. Motive and intention.

7 Knowledge, belief and verification   86

The nature of knowledge, belief and verification. Testing of belief through action.

8 Science: its scope and limits   93

The nature and practice of science. Technology and its power.

9 The organic analogy   105

The organic analogy; its origins in romanticism and its dangers when applied to human life and society. Kinship and nationalism.

10 Art as a way of knowing   114
The nature and practice of art. Contemplation in art.

11 The errors of individualism   124
Individualism and its dangers. The infant and mother.

12 The value of emotion   132
The neglect of emotion in our culture. Sentimentality.

13 Fear   140
Fear and its self-defeating nature. Fear against life.

14 Politics and law   146
The State, the law and the nature of democracy. Power as end in itself.

15 Morality   156
The nature of morality; sexual relationships.

16 Community   164
The nature of community. A common life.

17 The purpose of history   169
The nature of history as a discipline. History is intentional.

18 Greeks, Romans and Hebrews   173
The historical basis of European culture: Greeks, Romans and Hebrews.

19 Idealism   183
The false religion of idealism. God in this world.

20 Faith   192
The nature of faith.

21 Religion   196
The function of religion in human life. Religion and unreality.

22 God   204
Traditional arguments for the existence of God and their inadequacy.

23 The Meaning of Christianity   208
The meaning of Christianity in human history and its task for the future.

References   219

Select bibliography and further reading   221

Appendix   223
Organizations promoting the thought of John Macmurray.

To Robert Waller, with thanks

Foreword

by Tony Blair

John Macmurray is not one of the twentieth century's most famous philosophers. This is surprising. Actually his work is more accessible, better written and above all far more relevant than most of what I and many others studied as hallowed texts at university.

In the end, it is probable that his scope was too ambitious, too definitive for the narrow discipline of academic philosophers. For that reason alone, he is worth reading.

I also find him immensely modern. Not that all his thoughts and judgements did not betray the marks of his time. But rather, he was modern in the sense that he confronted what will be the critical political question of the twenty-first century: the relationship between individual and society. The first half of the twentieth century saw the creation of the great institutions of the collective will — the welfare state and government. The second half saw a reaction to them in the name of the individual who, partly through the power of government, had become more prosperous, was a taxpayer and developed a more individual-ized set of economic and social attitudes.

Now the task is to construct a new settlement for individual and society today. We have reached the limits of a narrow self-ish individualism; but have learnt the mistakes that collective power can make. We desire social stability and know there is an active role for government — the market is not master — but we want it for today, when culture, lifestyle and personal finances have been transformed.

Macmurray offers two insights. First, he places the individual firmly within a social setting — we are what we are, in part, because of the other, the 'You and I.' We cannot ignore our obligations to others as well as ourselves. This is where modern political notions of community begin.

Secondly, by rooting his vision in the personal world and in intention, he rejects simple determinism. The personal is not submerged in the social or organic.

In religious terms, also, it is easy to see his influence in a whole generation of Christian philosophers. For him, spirituality was based in this world; it was not an abstraction from it. Again, for many young people today, who search for spiritual meaning but who shrink from the notion it can be found in retreat from reason, Macmurray has much to say.

For philosophy to be at all relevant, it must either increase an understanding of the world or our ability to change it.

At best it can do both. This is a test John Macmurray passes with flying colours. I hope more people discover him.

Acknowledgments

I would like to express my grateful thanks to the following publishers:
Victor Gollancz, for permission to reprint extracts from *Christianity and the Social Revolution;*
Humanities Press, for permission to reprint extracts from *The Boundaries of Science, Conditions of Freedom, Constructive Democracy, Freedom in the Modern World, Interpreting the Universe, Persons in Relation, Reason and Emotion* and *The Self as Agent;*
Macmillan Publishers, for permission to reprint extracts from *Adventure;*
Routledge, for permission to reprint extracts from *Challenge to the Churches;*
SCM Press, for permission to reprint extracts from *Creative Society* and *The Clue to History;*
The Religious Society of Friends, for permission to reprint extracts from *The Philosophy of Jesus* and *Search for Reality in Religion;*
Yale University Press, for permission to reprint extracts from *The Structure of Religious Experience.*

I regret that I have been unable to trace ownership of the rights to *Idealism Against Religion, Religion, Art and Science* and *Some Makers of the Modern Spirit.*

I would also like to thank those who have helped me during the preparation of this anthology: Duncan Campbell, John Macmurray's literary executor; Father Jack Costello, S.J., of the John Macmurray Society; and Stanley M. Harrison, of Marquette University.

Michael Fielding, of the University of Cambridge Institute of Education, read and commented on the Introduction for me, and provided me with some pieces of bibliographical information.

Tony Blair found time in the midst of a demanding schedule to write the foreword; his generosity in this is greatly appreciated.

Finally, for his help, patience and encouragement, I would like to thank my editor at Floris Books, Christopher Moore. The idea for an anthology of John Macmurray's writings originated with Christopher, and I am very pleased to have been entrusted with the project and to have worked with him to see it through to completion.

PC

Introduction

If John Macmurray's name has had public exposure in the last two or three years, it is probably because his writings have influenced the Labour Party's leader Tony Blair. Madeleine Bunting, religious affairs editor of *The Guardian*, wrote on 6 October 1995:

> The Christian grounding for Mr Blair's politics was laid at Oxford where he was strongly influenced by an Australian mature theology student called Peter Thomson. In discussions which went late into the night a group of friends discussed the works of an English [sic] philosopher, John Macmurray. Mr Blair describes Mr Thomson ... as his spiritual mentor, but his intellectual inspiration was the very unfashionable philosopher.

Earlier in 1995 a writer in the *Sunday Telegraph* (30 July) wittily assumed that Tony Blair must have admired the film actor Fred Macmurray:

> But it turned out that Mr Blair meant Professor John Macmurray. He, it seems, was a Scottish philosopher.

He was indeed, and despite the dismissive tone one cannot greatly blame the writer for not having heard of him. It is a safe bet that the overwhelming majority of philosophy graduates in this country have never read a word of Macmurray, let alone studied him during their degree course. He rates a single footnote in John Passmore's *A Hundred Years of Philosophy*, being implicitly rejected as an eccentric Scot.[1] Yet none of this would have surprised Macmurray, who 'once remarked that even if he lived till the age of his mother, who died at 105, he did not expect to see his work accepted by a single trained philosopher.'[2]

Macmurray, who was born in 1891, would have been 105 this year, and his prediction has proved substantially correct. This is not to say that he has lacked influence, but the influence has been in fields other than academic philosophy; most notably in theology and psychology. Before we suggest some reasons why the academic world has neglected Macmurray, and consider how his thought might be applied to Britain's current social and cultural problems, let us look at his life and career.

The first chapter of this anthology gives a summary of Macmurray's early life, emphasizing his dual commitment, remarkable at the time, to both science and religion. When he entered the University of Glasgow in 1909 he wanted to be a scientist, but was persuaded to continue with Classics. Nevertheless, he arranged to take classes in Geology as well, a subject in which he was very successful. In 1913 he won an Exhibition award to Balliol College, Oxford. The outbreak of war the following year posed him an intense moral dilemma, as his religious faith inclined him to pacifism. After attempting a compromise by joining the Royal Army Medical Corps he became a lieutenant in the Cameron Highlanders. He was awarded the Military Cross, and was wounded at Arras in 1918. In 1916 he married Elizabeth Hyde, of Banchory.

Macmurray committed himself to philosophy because he believed that any civilization which could produce a débâcle like the Great War must be deeply flawed in its values and assumptions. As A.R.C. Duncan has put it:

> He preferred to think philosophically about problems
> which seemed to him to arise directly out of the life of
> the society in which he found himself living.[3]

Macmurray's scientific training made him aware of the link between ideas and action, and he applied this principle to societies, whose underlying ideas are verified or falsified by the extent to which they lead to human fulfilment or frustration.

Macmurray spent two years in South Africa, from 1919 to 1921, as Professor of Philosophy at the University of Witwatersrand, Johannesburg. It was probably during this period that he came into contact with J.C. Smuts' organic philosophy of Holism. Although Macmurray admired Smuts' work, and believed an organic interpretation of the world to be more adequate than a mechanistic one, he did not believe that human life could be understood organically, and devoted much of his subsequent career to rejecting such an interpretation (see Chapter 9).

In 1921 he returned to England as Fellow and Tutor at Balliol College, where he stayed for seven years. During this period he contributed to academic journals articles on a variety of subjects including art, Christianity, politics and science, and belonged to the Aristotelian Society, an élite forum of philosophical debate. During a conversation with me in 1972, he said that he had been in no hurry to publish a book, believing it unwise to do so before the age of forty in case too many qualifications and retractions then had to be made. He had preferred to undertake a thorough study of the history of philosophy before committing himself to any substantial thesis. However, it is clear from his contributions to the symposium *Adventure* that his ideas were beginning to take shape by 1927.[4]

Macmurray left Oxford in 1928 to become Grote Professor of Mind and Logic at University College, London. The 1930s were a period of immense activity for him, and although his crowning philosophical achievement, the Gifford Lectures of 1953–54, was still a long way ahead, he was at the height of his reputation during this time, far from the neglected and unfashionable figure he has since become. He gained a name — even notoriety — for himself with a series of broadcasts in 1930 which established him as one of the early intellectual influences on BBC radio. These talks, along with others given in 1932, were published as *Freedom in the Modern World,* which proved a very successful book over a long period, and is still an excellent introduction to Macmurray for the general reader.[5] Macmurray contributed regularly to BBC radio and its journal *The Listener* throughout the decade, and organized a broadcast symposium entitled 'Some Makers of the Modern Spirit' with Leonard Woolf and A.L. Rowse among the distinguished speakers.[6]

Another important event in the early 1930s was Macmurray's participation in J.H. Oldham's conference on the meaning of Christianity (see p.39). This led Macmurray to a detailed study of Marxism, on which he lectured and published books.[7] His interest in politics was not only theoretical. Believing as he did that religion is about the world we live in, and not about some ideal 'spiritual' world, he was a key figure in a group called Christian Left, which saw socialism as the logical conclusion for those wishing to apply Christian principles to politics. He supported Republican Spain and was a member of a delegation which visited there to report on events. (Hewlett Johnson, the 'Red Dean' of Canterbury, was a fellow member.) He was astute enough, however, to refuse an invitation to visit the Nazi leaders, for fear of seeming to give even the slightest tacit support to that régime. This practical commitment to political activity was to be continued during the Second World War, when Macmurray was a leading light, along with J.B. Priestley and Sir Richard Acland, in the Common Wealth Party, which attempted to keep some form of democracy alive by putting up socialist candidates against Coalition representatives.

During the 1930s Macmurray was also closely involved at one point with the literary critic John Middleton Murry and his Adelphi Centre in Essex, a forum for political and religious discussion. John Carswell describes Macmurray as a strong influence on Murry, and the novelist Rayner Heppenstall recalls Macmurray dominating the summer school of 1936. Others associated with the Adelphi Centre included George Orwell and the American philosopher Reinhold Niebuhr.[8]

Through his wife Betty, who was an artist, Macmurray knew the art critic Herbert Read, and he wrote a good deal during the 1930s on art and education. His book *Reason and Emotion* includes a number of pieces on these topics, including his Presidential Address to the Froebel Society. Macmurray lectured in the United States during the decade,[9] and his output of writing was at its most prolific (see Bibliography). Much of what he wrote was on politics and religion, but perhaps the most significant book for his development as a philosopher was *Interpreting the Universe,* published in 1933. In this work he analyses mechanistic and organic interpretations of life, arguing that they cannot do justice to human experience. He concludes that the century's chief philosophical task is to develop a logical form adequate to the nature of personality.

In 1944 Macmurray returned to his native Scotland to become Professor of Moral Philosophy at the University of Edinburgh, a post he held till his retirement in 1958. This move ensured, in effect, that he found himself on the sidelines of British philosophy, which was in any case moving in a very different direction from that which interested him.[10] As an expositor of philosophical ideas he remained outstanding, and his classes were very popular. He lectured in Canada in 1949,[11] and in Scotland was instrumental in ensuring the reopening in 1950 of Newbattle Abbey, a residential college for mature students.[12] He continued to produce academic articles and to give broadcast talks during the 1950s, and the year before he retired saw the publication of *The Self as Agent*, the first of two volumes outlining *The Form of the Personal*. The second, *Persons in Relation*, appeared in 1961. They were based on his Gifford Lectures at Glasgow, and mark the completion of the task he had set himself more than twenty years before. Academics in mainstream British philosophy took no notice; Macmurray was already largely forgotten.[13]

On his retirement Macmurray moved to Jordans, a Quaker village near Beaconsfield in Buckinghamshire, and the following year he became a member of the Society of Friends (Quakers). It was an appropriate decision for a man who sought a form of Christianity free from nationalism and dogma, and who had written in the Introduction to *The Form of the Personal*:

> All meaningful knowledge is for the sake of action, and
> all meaningful action for the sake of friendship.[14]

In retirement he did not disappear completely from the public eye: in November 1965 he was the subject of a *Viewpoint* programme on BBC television, chaired by Malcolm Muggeridge. Fellow guests in the discussion were the educationalist Kenneth Barnes, the Labour peer and Methodist preacher Dr Donald Soper and an anonymous psychiatrist.[15]

Macmurray lived at Jordans for more than ten years before returning to Edinburgh, where he remained until his death in June 1976 at the age of eighty-five.

We have seen that Macmurray had no influence on mainstream British philosophy. The guests on the *Viewpoint* programme referred to above indicate the areas where his influence is more likely to be discovered, the psychiatrist's presence being particularly significant. Macmurray's emphasis on personal relationships has appealed to various psychologists, including R.D. Laing and Aaron Esterson, Harry Guntrip, Karen Horney and Anthony Storr.[16] In the 1980s John Shotter, a lecturer at Nottingham University, based his study of psychology's philosophical foundations on Macmurray's work.[17] In retrospect we can see Macmurray's ideas as one strand in the development of psychologies of self-actualization, and of the 'anti-psychiatry' movement. Macmurray has also influenced theologians: the leading contemporary theologian Thomas Torrance is indebted

to Macmurray, and the late J.A.T. Robinson, who as Bishop of
Woolwich in the 1960s caused controversy with his widely read
book *Honest to God*, drew a great deal on Macmurray when
researching his doctorate on the Jewish philosopher Martin
Buber. The recently retired Archbishop of York, John Habgood,
is one of Macmurray's admirers, seeing his ideas as a corrective
to the individualism of our Conservative-dominated era.

A thinker who has been read by such a wide range of figures
can hardly be deemed to lack influence. Why, then, has Macmurray had so little impact on philosophy itself? David Fergusson suggests an answer when he describes him as:

> an ambitious writer who can never be accused of being
> too narrow in his interests or aspirations. He makes
> generalizations and presents high level hypotheses from
> which most modern philosophers would shrink ...[18]

As we have seen, Macmurray chose to concentrate on
philosophy as a result of his war experiences, in order to
examine the assumptions on which European civilization has
rested. The subject was important to him because he believed
ideas to have practical effects. Such a conception was entirely at
odds with the mood dominating British philosophy after 1945.
Macmurray's desire to create a philosophy adequate to human
experience through developing a new logical form was a world
away from logical positivism, Wittgenstein's 'language games'
or J.L. Austin's minutely pedantic verbal analysis. Similarly, his
avowed intention to re-establish philosophy as a form of 'natural
theology'[19] could hardly have been more remote from the secular
tone set by A.J. Ayer's view that all religious language is strictly
meaningless.[20] Oxford and Cambridge were the centres of
philosophy, and they allowed no place for anything which
smacked of metaphysics, system-building or, for that matter,
relevance to social issues. Macmurray believed that British philosophy had sacrificed content for the sake of method. In the 1965
Viewpoint programme he expressed sympathy for the existentialist view that thinking and doing must be closely linked, but
criticized the existentialists 'because of their carelessness about
philosophical form.'[21] (See Chapter 2.)

It would appear that Macmurray cannot be categorized,
standing as he does outside both the dominant British and European movements of the post-war years. However, I believe this

view mistaken, and that he can be considered the chief British representative of Personalism, a philosophical perspective at one time very influential, particularly in France. Emmanuel Mounier, the leading French exponent of Personalism, said that 'its central affirmation' was 'the existence of free and creative persons.'[22] The founder of the British Personalist group, J.B. Coates, defined Personalism as:

> the name given to a number of philosophies which correlate the conceptions of personality and value, which conceive of personality as a unique entity in every human being which has a movement towards value and is the source of our knowledge of value.[23]

'The name was born,' wrote Mounier, 'of a response to the expression of the totalitarian drive, against this drive, in order to stress the defence of the person against the tyranny of apparatus. From this aspect there was a risk of lining up with all the old reactionary individualism ... From the beginning, therefore, we were careful to associate with it the word "communal".'[24] The reason for this was that:

> if the 'we' is anterior to the 'one,' personal life is not a withdrawal upon the self, but a movement towards and with the other, towards and upon the material world, towards that which is above and beyond the realm of the given.[25]

And again:

> If there is one affirmation that is common to all the Personalist philosophies ... it is that the basic impulse in a world of persons is not the isolated perception of self (cogito) nor the egocentric concern for self, but the communication of consciousness ... the adult only finds himself in his relationship to others and to things, in work and comradeship, in friendship and in love, in action and encounter, and not in his relationship to himself.[26]

The parallels with Macmurray's thought are very marked in these extracts.[27]

It is not appropriate here to summarize Personalism in detail. The point to note is that Macmurray should be seen in the broad context of a European philosophical perspective which included among its representatives important figures such as Mounier, Gabriel Marcel, Max Scheler, Nicolas Berdyaev and Martin Buber. Macmurray does not refer to Mounier, but Mounier mentions Macmurray as an influence on Coates' group, which Mounier addressed in London in 1949. A few years earlier Macmurray had written the foreword to Coates' book *A Common Faith or Synthesis*.[28] The insularity of English philosophy in the post-war decades ensured that Macmurray became a marginal figure; though it might be more accurate to see English philosophy itself as marginal to the much more significant issues being dealt with in European thought. It would be almost impossible, from reading the linguistic philosophy dominant in British universities from the 1950s to the 1970s, to realize that during the previous half-century the world had been convulsed by revolution, totalitarianism and war.

Nevertheless, Macmurray did not, in addressing human problems, reject philosophical form and method. Indeed, his chief purpose was to find a new form capable of analysing personality, its modes of experience and its relatedness to both the material and the human world. This is why, however valuable, and at times inspirational, his other works may be, his Gifford Lectures must be seen as his outstanding achievement.

To say that the logical form Macmurray conceived is 'a positive which necessarily contains its own negative'[29] is unlikely in itself to encourage study of his works, but its abstract nature belies its productiveness as a seed-bed of ideas. Only a close study of *The Self as Agent* and *Persons in Relation*, the two volumes which make up *The Form of the Personal*, will reveal the intricacy and brilliance of Macmurray's thought in applying the form to all aspects of human life, and the extracts in this anthology can do no more than give relatively brief glimpses of the overall pattern.

Before we conclude by suggesting why Macmurray's thought is relevant to our present situation, a brief survey of what he tried to achieve is necessary.

All philosophical thought is by its nature theoretical, but Macmurray believed it possible to theorize from the standpoint of a material agent in a world of other material agents rather than from that of an isolated, purely thinking being, which was the origin of modern philosophy in Descartes' famous assertion, *'Cogito ergo sum:* I think, therefore I am.' Now, there is an im portant sense in which all Macmurray's philosophy is a philosophy of religion, and in his view Descartes' starting-point led inevitably to atheism. But since he considered atheism false, it followed that the Cartesian mode of thought must be mistaken. If the individual is no more than a detached consciousness, action becomes inexplicable and the existence of other people problematic: that of God, even more so. Here is the genesis of idealism, or dualism, to which Macmurray was im placably opposed: the splitting of experience into mind and matter, the spiritual and the secular, ideal freedom and material subservience to law (see Chapter 19). Religion, if not rejected outright as illusory, becomes a question of pure subjectivity, while the organization of everyday life is surrendered to scientists, managers and technocrats. In short, idealism breeds materialism.

Influenced by Kant's idea of 'practical reason,' Macmurray preferred to see knowledge as something gained through experience in action. Action — if it is to be action and not mere movement, response, or activity — necessarily involves the element of thought, a degree of conscious intention. It is therefore a more inclusive mode of experience than pure thought. One can, and should, periodically refrain from action in order to reflect, but such reflection becomes mere idealism unless tested in action. Furthermore, we act in a world of other agents. To claim to doubt that they exist, as Descartes did, is mere play: we owe our identity and very being to the existence of others. Macmurray argues that we cannot therefore think adequately if we see ourselves as isolated individuals. Analysis of our experience must acknowledge not just the discrete Self, but the more inclusive matrix of 'You and I.' The mind and the individual are abstractions, with no real independent existence.

Macmurray saw the history of philosophy since Descartes as falling into two phases. During the first of these, influenced by the achievements of the physical sciences, philosophers interpreted the world in terms of mechanism; during the second, as they responded to the rise of biological science, in terms of organism. Macmurray thought that the development of the human sciences should have led philosophers to interpret the world in terms of personality; instead the organic analogy continued to hold sway, with disastrous results in the political sphere (see Chapter 10). Macmurray's Form of the Personal includes as its negative (that is, non-personal) elements both the material and the biological nature of the person, but throughout his writings he insists that human life is distinct from the organic, being a matter not of evolution, but of conscious intention.

Macmurray's philosophy is markedly schematic, and science, art, and religion are the three chief modes of activity within the scheme. Science concerns itself with the 'world-as-means'; it brings knowledge of that which is constant in the world and of that which is predictable or habitual in human behaviour (see Chapters 6 and 8). Art is concerned with questions of value — the 'world-as-ends' — and with educating the senses and emotions (see Chapters 10 and 12). Religion is concerned with personal relations (see Chapter 21). Note that Macmurray sees science, art and religion as forms of action rather than as bodies of knowledge; but since they are forms of action they involve knowledge as an integral element of their performance. They are not rival forms of knowledge: they deal with different aspects of the world. In fact Macmurray reverses our dominant cultural assumptions by claiming that religion and art offer more complete forms of knowledge than science does. Religion gives the most complete knowledge of all because it deals with personal relationships and, as we have seen, Macmurray believed that the world can be fully understood only in terms of personality. Religion thus becomes, in his philosophy, something supremely *rational*, expressing as it does an awareness of our true nature as persons. Macmurray defined reason as our capacity for objectivity, and argued that our emotions are inherently no more irrational than our intellect: both can be educated (see Chapters 4 and 12). Since we do not exist as isolated beings, reason consists in fulfilling relationships with other persons, which it is the task of religion to achieve.

It was for this reason that Macmurray admired the Hebrew achievement which he saw as a recognition, first by the Prophets and then most fully by Jesus, of the personal nature of human life. While, like Marx, he rejected idealism, he did not believe religion, in any mature form, to be idealist, and argued that a study of the Hebrews, from whom Christianity derives, demonstrates this conclusively (see Chapter 18). In his view, the Hebrew tradition is concerned with progress towards a world community based on recognition of shared humanity and equal standing in relation to God. Such a hope involves rejecting the racialism implicit in any organic concept of human life, while belief in a personal God enables us to see history not as an impersonal evolutionary process, but as one action, through which eventual unity is sought.

However influential Macmurray may once have been, and however intellectually impressive his achievements, there is little point in recommending his thought unless it has something to say to us in our present circumstances. We can therefore conclude this Introduction by suggesting some areas to which his ideas have relevance.

In the early 1970s Martin Pawley wrote a book called *The Private Future*, in which he identified in western culture a 'voluntary abandonment of social obligation and community life' leading to a 'corresponding uninhabitability of what is left of a public realm dominated by bureaucracy and crime.' This 'pattern of private withdrawal' involves creation of a 'secondary reality' by means of technology and the media, consumer goods becoming 'tools for social disengagement.' Pawley prophetically used the term 'privatization' to describe what he saw developing, years before the word was used to indicate an entire political strategy.[30] If Pawley wanted to bring the book up to date, he could further strengthen his argument by referring to the ubiquity of personal stereos, the multiplying television channels, the invention of computerized 'virtual reality,' and the spread of neo-liberal political philosophy through the western and ex-communist worlds, with its consequent devaluing of nationalization, public ownership and socialized policies, its emphasis on individual 'choice,' and its competitive Social Darwinist ethic. The psychologist David Smail, in a recent book *The Origins of Unhappiness*, has analysed the same process at work in counselling and psychotherapy, which tend to ignore the social dimension to clients' problems and concentrate on purely individual methods of coping.[31]

The French Personalist Emmanuel Mounier insisted that Personalism is not the same as the individualism of liberal bourgeois ideology,[32] and Macmurray likewise attacked the individualist outlook (see Chapter 11). Freedom and fulfilment do not consist in escaping from other human beings or in withdrawing from social obligations: as persons, it is our nature to communicate and reciprocate, sharing in a common life.

Underlying every political philosophy is a view of human nature. The neo-liberalism which has afflicted Britain for a decade and a half was notoriously expressed by Margaret Thatcher when she declared that there is 'no such thing' as society. Personalist philosophy rejects this assumption, reminding us of the wider origins of our identity and arguing that any attempt to live in competition with, or isolation from, other persons is self-frustrating. Of course, we are free to frustrate ourselves, but we should not be misled into thinking that we are somehow fulfilling ourselves by doing so, or expect that a society based on such values will be a satisfying one in which to live.

One response to the effects of neo-liberalism has been the growth of communitarianism, a social philosophy developed by the American sociologist Amitai Etzioni, which aims to encourage:

> the reinvigorated community, the neighbourhood: those 'social webs of people who know one another ... and have a moral voice, who can draw on interpersonal bonds to encourage members to abide by shared values.'[33]

One can see here why Macmurray's ideas would attract communitarians, but the danger of communitarianism is that it might encourage a narrow, inward-looking conception of community — something small-scale, possessive of its identity and therefore potentially exclusive. In Macmurray's view, anything less than a world community is an incomplete expression of the truth about human life: that the equality of human beings as persons overrides all cultural and racial differences.

This brings us to another important feature of Macmurray's thought: that he disputes the validity of organic analogies applied to the personal aspect of human life. He insists that personal life is not mere matter of fact — of response to stimulus or of inevitable process — but is a matter of *intention*. The organic is the negative but essential aspect of personal life: personal life cannot exist without it, but it must not be identified with personal life. Similarly, human societies are sustained by conscious intention and cannot be accurately likened to organisms (see Chapter 9). Applied to society the organic analogy results in the totalitarian state.

David Smail has pointed out the dangers of relapsing into forms of behaviour which are biological rather than social:

> Fright, anger, superstition and suspicion are prominent among the basic biological characteristics which we have in common, and it is surely no accident that when social cohesion can no longer be maintained through common allegiance to culturally sophisticated and highly developed categories of meaning, one witnesses the emergence of aggressive, magical and paranoid forms of social order — as for example in genocidal racialism, religious fanaticism and other forms of association round fundamentally irrational but emotionally highly charged systems of meaning. These do not stretch out in any attempt to engage with the complexities of a real environment, but rather reach back to cohere around the primitive physical engines of emotion which we all share ...[34]

A biological view of humanity attaches importance to race and breeding; a personal view recognizes that humans can create relationships and societies which transcend biological differences. We live in a time not only of resurgent liberalism but of resurgent fascism, and Macmurray's emphasis on the dangers of the organic analogy is salutary.

Macmurray's philosophy opposes all forms of reductionism. Although it does not deny the importance of the mechanical and the organic, it argues that to interpret human activities in these terms is to *abstract* from our completeness as persons. It follows that human activities are rational and valid only to the extent that they are for the sake of personal life and help to enrich it. The contemporary emphasis on management techniques and business models of efficiency, for instance, is irrational because it turns what is only a means into an end in itself, destroying the quality of personal and social life as it does so. Anyone who works in the health service or in education, to name but two areas infected by the managerial obsession, will be familiar with the way in which the concerns of the person are rendered secondary to impersonal systems. This is reductionism in practice, and its presuppositions require challenging by a philosophy which reasserts the primacy of the person.

Such practices are often justified, despite their evident folly,

on grounds of unsentimental rationality, while their opponents
are criticized for being 'emotive.' Macmurray, by separating the
concept of 'reason' from that of 'intellect,' provides a means of
counter-attack. The cold, detached technical or managerial
intellect may be thoroughly *ir*rational; emotions are not irrational
in themselves and indeed may be objectively appropriate to a
situation and therefore, in Macmurray's terms, completely
rational (see Chapters 4 and 12). Macmurray's rescue of the
emotions from their exile in the realms of the irrational is not
the least valuable of his achievements, and has significant implications for education, where a greater importance would need
to be given to the arts (see Chapter 10).

This Introduction began with a reference to Macmurray's
influence on the Labour Party leader Tony Blair. While one
would not wish to make an assessment of Macmurray's philosophy depend on the success or otherwise of any possible
Labour Government, it is worth noting by way of conclusion the
significance in this context of Macmurray's views on religion.
The Rt Rev Graham Dow, Bishop of Willesden, has praised Tony
Blair for:

> bringing God back into politics ... There are a great many
> Christians who have been very uneasy about the
> government of the last sixteen years.[35]

Yet when Margaret Thatcher became Prime Minister in 1979
she quoted St Francis of Assisi as the supposed inspirer of
her approach to government, and evidently considered herself
to be in some sense a Christian. According to Shirley Robin
Letwin:

> The fundamental postulate of Thatcherism is ... that
> human beings are and should be treated as self-moving
> makers of their own destinies [since] it is a central tenet
> of Christian doctrine, *at least in some versions*, that each
> person is an immortal soul who has to answer to God for
> what he makes of himself ... This view of Christianity
> underlies the British morality and renders it both
> sceptical and individualistic.[36] [my italics]

We see here the common identification of Christianity with two
of Macmurray's chief targets: individualism and idealism. The

social world becomes an atomized secular arena of competing beings, ruled by supposedly unalterable economic laws, any attempts to soften which are merely sentimental; while religion is reduced to a private matter of the individual soul's balance sheet. The etherialization of religion into a diffuse 'spirituality' likewise serves the interests of the powers that be, by deflecting any dissatisfaction with life into channels which are compensatory and escapist, or which may even enable people to serve the world of economic materialism more comfortably. Macmurray's view of religion emphasizes its nature as common activity in the world of embodied human beings; its concern should be to transform those conditions which frustrate our completeness as persons.

Macmurray's philosophy is nothing if not ambitious. It aims to present an entirely new logical form and reverse the direction taken by philosophy since Descartes; to make the discipline relevant to contemporary social and cultural problems; to re-think fundamental concepts like reason and emotion; to reinterpret the meaning of Christianity and its effect on western society; and to present science, art and religion as valid modes of knowledge which do not conflict with each other. Such a wide-ranging thinker is bound to be challenged in many areas, and since his analysis of the Form of the Personal is exploratory, there will no doubt be many differing views on its implications for the various fields to which it is applied. Malcolm Muggeridge, introducing the *Viewpoint* programme on Macmurray in 1965, remembered him as an intellectual influence on the radio and said of his talks:

> I was too much of a Marxist in those days fully to appreciate his efforts to reconcile Marxism and Christianity. Now perhaps I'm too much of a Christian to fully appreciate them.[37]

This comment incisively identifies one seemingly inevitable conflict between Macmurray's admirers, and one can also foresee different feminist responses to his ideas on sexual matters, and on the mother–child relationship. Equally, though, the comprehensive nature of his work means it will have insights to offer to most readers, whether in the sphere of religion, politics, science, art, education, or philosophy itself.

In any case, perhaps the importance of a philosophical work

does not, finally, lie in whether we can agree with all that it says, but in whether it impresses us as a coherent intellectual achievement fertile enough to encourage reflection on its pro- positions. In this respect, the thought of John Macmurray thoroughly deserves the interest it is at last beginning to attract.

Philip Conford
January 1996
Chichester

Editor's Note

Although John Macmurray was a professional philosopher, much of what he wrote was aimed at a non-specialist readership. This anthology has been organized according to topics, with no attempt made to group the various extracts according to their degree of philosophical difficulty, and readers may therefore find the tone and approach of one passage noticeably different from that which precedes or follows it.

Certain sections are predominantly or even entirely academic in their content: the extracts on 'Unity-patterns' are an example, and may appear somewhat daunting to readers who are not familiar with philosophy. All readers are, of course, free to dip into the selections as they choose, but the full range and complexity of Macmurray's thought cannot be grasped without an appreciation of the philosophical task which dominated his career; an understanding of what he meant by 'unity-patterns' is fundamental to this.

For the general reader the best introductions to Macmurray are probably *Freedom in the Modern World* and *Religion, Art and Science.* Those who are particularly interested in his religious thought will find a succinct summary of it in *Search for Reality in Religion.* For an accessible introduction to his ideas on community *Conditions of Freedom* is recommended. *Interpreting the Universe* is more rigorously academic, though still a comparatively straightforward outline of his philosophical concerns.

However, the one work which embodies the thought of John Macmurray most comprehensively is his two-volume set of Gifford Lectures (1953–54), *The Form of the Personal,* comprising *The Self as Agent* and *Persons in Relation.* Parts of this — of the first volume especially — are very demanding, and not for the intellectually faint-hearted. Those who persevere will find many rewards, not the least of which is the sense of watching a pattern emerge, broad in scope and intricate in detail. For this reason, more material has been drawn from the Gifford Lectures than from any of Macmurray's other writings. They have recently been reissued in Britain by Faber and Faber, and I hope that this anthology will stimulate the reader to investigate them in their entirety.

Abbreviations

The following abbreviations indicate the titles and editions of the books from which extracts are taken.

A   *Adventure: The Faith of Science and the Science of Faith,* B.H. Streeter, C.M. Chilcott, J. Macmurray, and A.S. Russell; Macmillan, London 1927.

BS   *The Boundaries of Science: a Study in the Philosophy of Psychology,* Faber, London 1939.

CC   *Challenge to the Churches: Religion and Democracy,* Kegan Paul, London 1941.

CD   *Constructive Democracy,* Faber, London 1943.

CF   *Conditions of Freedom,* Faber, London 1950.

CH   *The Clue to History,* SCM Press, London 1938.

CS   *Creative Society: a Study of the Relation of Christianity to Communism,* SCM Press, London 1935.

CSR   *Christianity and the Social Revolution,* ed. J. Lewis, K. Polanyi, and D.K. Kitchin; Gollancz, London 1935.

FMW   *Freedom in the Modern World* [1932], Faber, London (2nd edn) 1935.

IAR   *Idealism Against Religion,* Lindsey Press, London 1944.

ITU   *Interpreting the Universe,* Faber, London 1933.

PJ   *The Philosophy of Jesus,* Friends Home Service Committee, London 1973.

PR   *Persons in Relation* (Vol.2 of *The Form of the Personal*), Faber, London 1961.

RAS   *Religion, Art and Science: a Study of the Reflective Activities in Man,* Liverpool University Press, 1961.

RE   *Reason and Emotion* [1935], Faber, London, 2nd edn, 1962.

SAA   *The Self as Agent* (Vol.1 of *The Form of the Personal*), Faber, London 1957.

SMMS   *Some Makers of the Modern Spirit: a Symposium,* Methuen, London 1933.

SRE   *The Structure of Religious Experience,* Faber, London 1936.

SRR   *Search for Reality in Religion,* Allen & Unwin, London 1965.

– 1 –

Autobiographical

John Macmurray became a member of the Society of Friends (Quakers) in 1959. In 1965 he was invited to give the Society's annual Swarthmore Lecture, for which he chose the title Search for Reality in Religion. *The first section of the lecture is an autobiographical account of his early years, his experiences during the First World War, and his consequent commitment to the study of philosophy.*

In the following extracts we can see emerging the main concerns of his philosophical writings: the central importance of religious faith and the need to ensure its rootedness in common human experience; the need for experimental truth in religion as well as in science; the conviction that philosophical assumptions are verified or falsified historically through their effects on the societies which they underlie. Like many men who survived the horrors of the trenches, Macmurray concluded that there was something fundamentally wrong with a view of life which could lead to such disaster, and he reacted against the ideas and hypocrisies of the previous generation.

I was fortunate to be born into a deeply religious family. My parents were at one in a Christian piety which dictated the form of family life and determined its atmosphere. Its earliest component was the traditional Calvinism of the Scottish Church. This is perhaps the most intellectual of the Christian traditions, with the central stress falling upon soundness of doctrine; with the Bible as the inspired book of reference in any dispute. I can remember the incredulous amazement with which, later on, I heard an English scholar distinguish science and religion as the expressions respectively of the intellectual and the emotional aspects of human consciousness. The centre of my own religious upbringing had been instruction in organized correctness of doctrine, coupled with a distrust and suppression of emotion in favour of the revealed truth. With this went a strict morality expressed in rules and prohibitions, which was itself referred to

the authority of scripture and was taken for granted as universally binding. So my religious training made me familiar with
theology from an early age and encouraged the systematic study
of scripture.

SRR 5f

... while still at school, in the revivalist fervour that followed the
mission of Torrie and Alexander, I began to take part regularly
in evangelistic activities. I formed a group of boys of my own
age, who met weekly in each other's houses for Bible study and
prayer. I addressed evangelistic meetings, mostly in the open air.
I served as assistant evangelist to a tent mission in Aberdeen-
shire. I spoke occasionally in the meeting for worship. In all this
I was earnest, and in the ordinary and superficial sense, sincere.
Looking back upon it, however, I think that all this religious
activity was second-hand and somewhat priggish. It was the
result of the teaching of others, absorbed and elaborated by a
quick and busy mind, rather than the expression of a personal
religious experience. In spite of its seriousness and conviction,
it was religiously unreal. From this I learned, in the end, how
easy it is for religious convictions, in spite of the sincerity and
passion with which they are entertained and expressed, to be
imitative and imaginary, the products of a romantic sentimentality, or the symbols of pressures in oneself which are not
themselves religious. At the same time, I found myself unable
to question the reality of the religious experience of my parents,
even when the forms of its expression, particularly in doctrine
and belief, became more and more incredible to me. It was a
long time before I was able to draw the full conclusion from this
and to make it fundamental, as it must be, to any religious
understanding. It is this. The dichotomy which governs religious
experience is one between real and unreal. This is not identical
with the intellectual distinction between true and false; nor with
the aesthetic distinction between what satisfies or does not
satisfy our emotions, even if it is related to these. For it is possible for us to have a real religious experience coupled with
religious beliefs and practices which are fallacious and undesir-
able; or to hold sincerely and convincedly to religious beliefs
and practices with no reality to sustain them.

      This statement, of course, represents a point of view that I
could only formulate very much later. If I set it out here it is to
indicate my belief that it was already implicit in my earliest

experience. As soon as I began serious reflection on my religious position, it began to show itself, and as the years went by it became more and more evident. But if I now return to a fully factual statement, I might say this. I was convinced that religion had its own reality, so firmly that I have never afterwards been able to question it for a moment. This came from the knowledge of the quality of religious life in my parents; and is the most valuable thing that they gave me. Other important things which remained with me were a thorough knowledge of the Bible, both Old and New Testaments; a good grasp of the major principles of traditional Protestant theology, and of the issues which separated the Protestant churches from the Roman church, and some practical experience of religious activities, particularly evangelistic activities, and the ideas and attitudes which underlie them.

Before I go on to record the important religious changes during the second stage of my life — as a student and as a soldier — there is one developing interest of my childhood and schooldays which, though not religious, must be mentioned here, because of the future influence it was to have upon my religious development. This was an early and continuing interest in science. It began, before I had reached my teens, with astronomy. Ball's *Starland* was my textbook, and it came to me as a revelation. It was followed by a strong interest in biology, so that during my schooldays I read every book that I could find on the plant and animal life of the world. If I had had my own way I should have become a scientist. But headmasters and directors of studies were too strong for me, and my father, in spite of his own belief in education, did not feel competent to decide, against the advice of the teachers, between a classical and a modern curriculum. The schoolmasters had their eyes upon bursary competition and university entrance. My director of studies at Glasgow University, convinced of the superiority of a classical education and the crudity of science as an educational instrument, insisted that I should not sacrifice what I had already gained at school. In both cases I fought a successful rearguard action by winning concessions. I was allowed to include science, both at school and at my first university, as an extra subject in a classical course. At school it was chemistry; at the university, geology. The first provided a sound basis for widening private studies which have continued sporadically throughout my life. The latter provided a first-rate training in various branches of science and their practical applications. Geology has the advantage, in spite of the specialization which science requires, that it must use the help and the techniques of other branches of scientific study. My university course included not merely field-work and microscopic examination, but mineralogy, crystallography, palaeontology, as well as geological map-making and laboratory work in the determination of minerals. I was the only arts student in a large class of pure and applied scientists and mining engineers, and it was the only university class in which I carried off the medal. This solid grounding in science and scientific method has been of the greatest possible use to me not only as a philosopher in a country where few philosophers have any direct experience of science but at least as much in the religious field. For the question of the relation between science and religion has been dominant during my lifetime, and has not merely turned large numbers of intelligent people against religion, but issued in unending controversies and apologetics on behalf of one and the other. In these discussions I have been constantly struck by the ignorance displayed on both sides. The more general impression which I carried away from my scientific studies, however, was that science is far easier than any of the humanistic studies and especially than philosophy. This is, I suspect, a major reason for its astonishing success in our time.

SRR 8–12

The rest of my religious development, which was gradual and slow, can best be expressed with reference to a few key points which crystallized its various stages. The first of these happened during the first year of my university studies. I had agreed to conduct a Bible Class for young men of my own age, or a little older, at the Glasgow Mission Hall which I attended. I decided that we would study the Epistle of Paul to the Romans. I made this choice because, as I had been taught, the tap root of Christian theology was to be found here. In my classical studies I had been learning techniques for dealing with ancient texts by way of analysis and comparison, which could, if properly used, lay bare their meaning. I decided, in preparation for my class, to apply these methods to the Epistle to the Romans. I knew, of course, the theological use to which the early chapters were put, as sources of central doctrines. But I put these out of my mind so far as possible, and concentrated upon an analysis of the text as if it were new and unknown to me. The result was startling.

I discovered, after checking and rechecking my work, that these great doctrines of the Christian faith just were not there. Their attachment to the text of the Epistle depended upon what seemed to me to be a misunderstanding. Two things about it, however, were decisive. The first was that the theology in which I had been trained could not stand up to a scientific scrutiny of the scriptural text from which it claimed to be derived. This did not result in a rejection of theology, far less of religion itself. But it made theology questionable and so destroyed its dogmatic claims. I did reject *dogma*, in the belief that theology required critical analysis and reconstruction. The second decisive result came from the consciousness that I was using scientific tools to test the validity of my religious beliefs. This had the effect of associating science in general with my religious development, and so saved me from the tension between science and religion which drove so many of my contemporaries out of Christian belief altogether. In the scientific field, I thought, one does not throw science overboard because a favourite theory has been shown to be invalid. Why should it be different in religion? Could we not hope that through testing and modification we should arrive at a religion which science need not be ashamed to serve?

SRR 13f

With me [the war] resulted in a quick and complete acceptance of death, for myself as well as for my comrades. It had seemed a dreaded end, before the war. Now it became an incident in life, and in the result it removed for ever the *fear* of death. This is a tremendous gain in reality; for until we reach it — however we do reach it — we cannot see our life as it really is, and so cannot live it as we should. The fear of death is the symbol in us of all fear; and fear is destructive of reality. It is true that one can gain this familiarity with death and use it falsely. We can say, as so many of my contemporaries did after the war, 'Let us eat and drink, for tomorrow we die.' But it may just as well lead us to the opposite conclusion. We may feel that life is precious because it is short; and because it may end at any moment we must live so that every day would be a good day to die in, if death should come. Without this knowledge of death, I came to believe, there can be no real knowledge of life and so no discovery of the reality of religion.

In the second place, I should set, as the product of this new experience, the process of gradual disillusionment which I shared with so many of my comrades in arms. We went into war in a blaze of idealism, to save little Belgium and to put an end to war. We discovered, stage by stage, what childish nonsense all this idealism was. We learned that war was simply stupidity, destruction, waste and futility. We became critical, sceptical and sometimes cynical. By the end of it, we knew that war could never achieve what those who chose it expected it to achieve. It was inherently destructive and wasteful — of life, of time, of a thousand possibilities, as well as of the means of life — of homes and all the hard-won machinery of living. It could stop things — like the plans of the Kaiser — but it could construct nothing. I knew enough of history to realize that the great forward steps in human progress had in most cases been the results of warfare — but not the *intended* results; and the major result of the war in which I fought was wholly unintended — the setting up of communism in Russia.

So by the end of the war we soldiers had largely lost faith in the society we had been fighting for. We felt that we had been 'led up the garden path' by the powers that be; that our young enthusiasm and trust and ignorance had been played upon by men whose real interest was in their own wealth and power and prestige. We believed that our leaders were either rascals or blind leaders of the blind. Our eyes were opened. I can still remember how I heard the first post-war House of Commons described from inside as a collection of 'hard-faced men who looked as though they had done well out of the war.' I said to myself, 'That's what *we* thought; and it seems we were right.' So it came about that with hundreds of thousands of others I came out of the Great War saying, 'Never again!'

There is one incident belonging to this war-time experience to which I must refer, because it had a decisive influence upon my future religious life. I had been a year and a quarter in France before I had leave to go home for a few days. When I found myself, after this long time, again in civilian surroundings and amongst civilians, I was shocked by the change in their attitude of mind. I felt as though an evil spirit had entered into them, a spirit of malice and hatred. Before twenty-four hours had passed I wanted to get back to the trenches, where for all the misery and destruction, the spiritual atmosphere was relatively clean. It was, I think, the ignorant and superstitious hatred of the Germans, and the equally ignorant and unreal glorification of us, in the trenches, as heroes that had this effect. In France we were not heroes, nor expected to be; and we did not hate Germans, at least not the Germans in the trenches opposite. We understood them, and they understood us. We were sharing the same spurious and obscene life, no doubt with the same feelings. They had been dumped into war, no doubt, as we had, so we had a fellow-feeling for our enemies, which showed itself in odd little ways. I remember one night in the front-line, where we had been enjoying a quiet time, with a Saxon regiment opposite. We had been carrying on our war on the principle, 'Don't bother us and we won't bother you.' On this night a Saxon soldier on patrol slipped over to our trench and dropped a card on us. It read — in English — 'Watch out! The Prussians are taking over tomorrow.' A gulf had been fixed, it seemed, between ourselves and our friends and acquaintances in civilian life. We had ceased to understand one another. I can remember feeling, as I returned from this short leave — during which, indeed, I had got married — that now most of the pacifists were in the trenches.

This was in October, 1916. I had not been long back on the Somme battlefield when I was incapacitated by spraining an ankle. I was only three weeks in hospital in England before I was released on sick-leave, and it was some months before I was able to return to France. During this period I was asked to preach, in uniform, in a church in North London. I took the opportunity to advise the church and the Christians in it, to guard against this war-mentality; and to keep themselves, so far as possible, aloof from the quarrel, so that they would be in a position — and of a temper — to undertake their proper task as Christians when the war was over, of reconciliation. The congregation took it badly; I could feel a cold hostility menacing me; and no one spoke to me when the service was over. It was after this service that I decided, on Christian grounds, that I should never, when the war was over, remain or become a member of any Christian church. I kept to this resolve all my life as a university teacher. It was only after my retirement that I applied for membership of the Society of Friends. (But even during the war, though my knowledge of Quakerism was indirect and impersonal, I had made an exception in its favour because of its attitude to war.) I was not, however, tempted to abandon religion. I justified my refusal to join a religious organization to myself — I had no desire to make a parade of it

— as a personal Christian protest against a spurious Christianity. I spoke and wrote thereafter in defence of religion and of Christianity; but I thought of the churches as the various national religions of Europe.

When I left the army and my university studies in 1919, it was without any religious attachment, with a suspicion about the validity of theology, and as a confirmed realist. I had shed the idealism of my pre-war outlook. I had gained a purpose in life; for when I said 'Never again!' I meant it as a dedication to the elimination of war from human life. Whatever sphere of activity I might find myself involved in — and my hope then was that it might be on the staff of the new 'League of Nations' — I intended to use it to this end. When it appeared that I was to spend my life in teaching philosophy, this became the underlying purpose of all my philosophizing. To this task I brought a mind that had become deeply sceptical of the principles underlying the European civilization in which I had been brought up and which had issued in the savage destruction and stupid waste in which I had played my part. Convinced that the source of error must be deeply hidden, I decided, as a rule to guide my search for it, to distrust and question especially those principles of whose truth I should find my elders most unshakeably convinced.

So far as concerned religion I was still a convinced Christian with no doubt that the religious issue was the most central and most important of all issues. But I had given up all the churches; I had turned from the past and was looking to the future, believing that Christianity had to be rediscovered and recreated. When I asked myself, as I did, why I had given up the churches, and why so many of my contemporaries had given up religion by identifying it with the churches, the answer I found for myself and for them was that we could no longer believe in their *bona fides;* that they did not mean what they said; so that what they said, even if it were true, had become irrelevant. I still consider that this is what stands between the world and the church — this question of bad faith — and not intellectual difficulties about outdated myths or cosmologies. The difficulties are no longer intellectual or theoretical at all. They are *moral.* For very many of my generation, and for even more of the younger generations that have followed us, there hangs about the official representative of religion an odour, not of sanctity, but of disingenuousness. This feeling may be false. But it can only be proved false, I imagine, by a dramatic action that demonstrates its falsity in a manner which cannot be gainsaid or ignored.

SRR 18–23

In about 1930 Macmurray was invited to a conference, organized by the theologian J.H. Oldham, on the nature of Christianity. (T.S. Eliot, who in his capacity as a director of Faber and Faber was soon to become Macmurray's publisher, also attended.) As a result of this conference Macmurray began to study Marx's early writings, and to engage with Marx's rejection of religion.

The positive phase of my religious development, which has occupied the whole of my maturity and is still incomplete, has been an effort to discover the *reality* of religion, by answering the question, 'What is Christianity?' It was only many years later, when the main lines of my answer had been laid down, that I discovered how closely my own story repeated, a century later, that of Søren Kierkegaard. I might have expressed my own problem in his terms as the problem 'How to become a Christian.' There were, of course, great differences. How could it be otherwise a century later? As a philosopher I could not see the Hegelian system as the summing up of all philosophy. As a religious seeker, I could not, as he did, take the major doctrines of traditional theology for granted, and as a student of social history I could not accept the radical individualism of his attitude and of his answers. I found myself in these things much closer to the prophetic insight of one of the very greatest of modern thinkers, Martin Buber. But the shape of Kierkegaard's problem and of mine were much the same. For both of us the problem took the form that he taught us to label 'existential.' There was, however, one occasion which had such a marked effect both in illuminating and enlarging the problem and in redirecting my search for a solution, that it should, perhaps, be included. I was invited to take part in a private conference in London. I found on arrival that my fellow members were representatives of the various Churches for the most part, all of them leaders in their own fields and many of them well known in the country beyond the limits of their own profession. Besides those there were a few men who, like myself, were not churchmen, but laymen with religious interests. What the subject of our conference was to be we did not know until our first meeting, when our host, himself one of the outstanding religious leaders of my generation, suggested that we should discuss the question, 'What is Christianity?' We did this for the whole of that day, and in the evening we came to the unanimous conclusion that we did not know. The next day we went on to ask how we could find out; and after a long discussion we concluded that before we could discover what Christianity is we should have to study seriously two other questions. The first of these was the nature of modern Communism, the other was the problem of sex. We then decided that we would tackle Communism first, and appointed one of our number to write a paper about Communism and Christianity which should be the basis of discussion for a later meeting.

It was this conference which led me to undertake a thorough study of the early writings of Karl Marx, with an eye to discovering, in particular, the historical relation between Marxism and the Christian tradition. I was astonished to find how close the relation was and how correct the conviction of the conference was that the study of Communism was a necessary prelude to the understanding of Christianity. I, at least, found that I learned a great deal about Christianity by this study, and especially by coming to understand the reasons behind Marx's rejection of religion. The basic reason was his conviction that religion was the popular, and therefore the important form of idealism,* and his rejection of religion was the most serious aspect of his attack upon idealism. My critique of this was so important in my own religious development that I can best complete this section of my lecture by summarizing its conclusion.

I was wholly convinced by Marx that idealism is a dangerous illusion which must be rejected. But I was not convinced that religion is necessarily a form of idealism. In particular, the Hebrew religion, as it appears in the Old Testament, is not idealistic at all. On the other hand, a great deal of what passes for Christianity is undoubtedly idealist, and must either be cured of its idealism or rejected. As this thought developed in my mind I became convinced that idealism and religion are, in the end, incompatible with one another. Their identification by Marx is the basic error of Marxism. Idealist religion is *unreal*. Marx

---

*   *Idealism.* Wherever the spiritual life is dissociated from the material life, and is valued and pursued for its own sake, we have idealism. The opposite of idealism is the integration of theory and practice, not in theory but in practice. The most obvious expression of idealism in religion is, perhaps, otherworldliness. [Macmurray's footnote.]

would have been justified in calling for the reform of religion
but not for its rejection. Yet this would have led to a wholly
different understanding of human society from the communist
one. When I looked for the cause of the idealizing of Christianity, I found it in the acceptance by the church of the Roman
Empire. This 'acceptance' was a long process, though it may
seem short by compression when we look back through the
centuries. It includes the process by which, under the influence
of Greek philosophy, the effort was made to determine an
orthodoxy of belief and to extirpate heresy; and equally the
process which led to the creation of a hierarchical and authoritarian church parallel to and modelled to some extent upon the
organization of the Roman State. The first of these implies a
theoretical, or Greek, conception of Christianity; the second a
Roman or legal conception of the Church. The 'adoption' of
Christianity by Constantine in the early fourth century is a
useful date to remember, but, of course, people are not made
Christian by the decree of an Emperor. In becoming the religion
of the Roman Empire the Church was logically bound to
distinguish between the spiritual and the material realms, and
to recognize the ordering of the latter as the proper sphere of
the State. The function of the Church had to become, in effect,
whatever the theory might be, a purely spiritual one. A purely
spiritual religion is necessarily an idealist religion, and so unreal.
For the purely spiritual is the purely imaginary. It seemed,
indeed, that modern Communism might well be that half of
Christianity which had been dropped by the Church in favour
of an accommodation with Rome, coming back to assert itself
against the part that had been retained.

SRR 23–27

– 2 –

The task of philosophy

Macmurray found himself unable to accept either of the two main philosophical trends of the post-war decades. In England the dominant figures were A.J. Ayer (Macmurray's successor at University College, London), Gilbert Ryle, J.L. Austin, and Wittgenstein. Metaphysics was rejected in favour of linguistic analysis. On the continent the new schools of existentialism and phenomenology were influential. In Macmurray's view, English philosophy abandoned the traditional content of philosophy and concentrated on the formal method, while European philosophy addressed the essential issues but abandoned the method. His intention was to deal with those issues through the established philosophical methods, thereby preserving the subject as a distinct and significant form of intellectual endeavour.

We need only recognize the break with tradition which is apparent in all fields in our own society — in religion and morals, in politics and economics, and in the arts. In such circumstances we should expect to find a break in the continuity of philosophical development, a radical criticism of traditional philosophy and a search for new ways and new beginnings. And this we do find. We need only think of such developments as phenomenology, logical empiricism or existentialism to realize that new modes of philosophy are being created and spreading rapidly, which stand in strong contrast with the main stream of traditional thought. The first of these is confessedly an effort to start afresh where Descartes started, but employing a catharsis of the mind to remove prejudice and achieve an innocence of immediate vision for whatever can be object for thought. Logical empiricism, armed with a high-powered analytic technology, is concerned to make an end of all metaphysics, and to include under metaphysics most of what has traditionally been considered the substance of philosophical doctrine. Its main interest in the past is to show how it was constantly led, not into error, but into meaningless debate by failure to perform the only proper task of philosophy, the logical analysis of language. Existentialism, on the other hand, has so altered the focus of attention, and so largely turned its back upon the established methods of procedure that many have doubted its claim to be a philosophical discipline at all.

These two contemporary forms of philosophy, logical empiricism and existentialism, represent, it would seem, opposite reactions to the breakdown of the tradition. They are united in the extremity of their difference, not merely by their negative attitude to the philosophical past, but if I mistake not, by a common conviction from which both arise. I may express this roughly by saying that both rest upon the decision that the traditional method of philosophy is incapable of solving its traditional problems. But whereas the logical empiricists discard the problems in order to maintain the method, the existentialists relinquish the method in wrestling with the problems. So the latter achieve a minimum of form; the former a minimum of substance. The logical empiricists are content to elaborate the subtleties of formal analysis — and often with the beauty of genius; so far as the substantial problems go, they use their formalism to erect notices on every path which say 'No road this way!' For all the roads that do not lead to the impassable bogs of metaphysics belong to the special sciences. The existentialists, determined to grapple with the real problems — and their sensitiveness to the darkness of human despair leads them to discover the emergent problem of our time — find no formal analysis that is adequate to the task. They are constrained to quit the beaten track; to wallow in metaphor and suggestion; to look to the drama and the novel to provide an expression, albeit an aesthetic expression, for their discoveries.

Where is the way forward? Do we go along with one of these contemporary schools of thought? Or should we count them as aberrations engendered by the stress and sickness of our age, and hold to the beaten paths of traditional thought? My own answer to this decisive question is as follows. We *cannot* keep to the old ways. The tradition is broken, and cannot be re-established. It is true, as the new movements imply, that the traditional methods cannot answer the traditional questions. Form and matter, in philosophy, have parted company. Then what of the new modes? Phenomenological analysis is a useful device. We can be grateful for it, and use it when we find it helpful. But if it is taken as more than this; if it means that we go back to Descartes and the modern starting-point and do properly what we have so far done poorly, we must answer that there is no going back. History does not repeat itself. Yet when I turn to choose between the other two schools, I find I can accept neither. To the logical empiricists I find I must say this: 'Philosophy, like any branch of serious reflective inquiry, is created and defined by its problems; and its problems are not accidental, but necessary; grounded in the nature of human experience. If I find that my method of attempting to answer them is unsuccessful, if it fails even to discover a meaning in them, then I must conclude that there is something wrong with the method, and seek a better one. To discard the problems in order to retain the method; to seek for problems which the method *could* solve, would be neither serious nor reasonable.' To the existentialists I should say this: 'Philosophy, as you would agree, is an intellectual discipline. It is therefore necessarily formal and must work through concepts which seek for clarity and exact definition both in themselves and in their systematic interrelation. It is right to hold firmly to the substantial problems, however metaphysical and elusive, which form the centre of gravity of the philosophic enterprise. It is an important contribution to the progress of the enterprise to trace them to their origins in the strains and stresses of the personal life. But if this results in the dissolution of the formal structures of traditional philosophy, what is required is the search for a new form which shall be not less but more logical and intellectual than the inadequate forms that have to be discarded.' We may sum up this estimate of these two emergent philosophical tendencies in a sentence, even though, like all such judgments, it must need qualification in detail. Existentialism has discovered, with sensitiveness of feeling, that the philosophical problem of the present lies in a crisis of the personal: logical empiricism recognizes it as a crisis of logical form and method. Both are correct, and both are one-sided. The cultural crisis of the present is indeed a crisis of the personal. But the problem it presents to philosophy is a formal one. It is to discover or to construct the intellectual form of the personal.

SAA 26–29

The problem facing modern philosophy

I have referred to the form of the personal as the emergent problem of contemporary philosophy, and this requires both to be explained and to be justified. For it is far from being the case that this is the problem with which philosophy is particularly concerning itself at present. What is meant is rather that the historical situation in which we find ourselves presents us with a philosophical problem for solution, and that this problem concerns the form of the personal. The decisive questions of serious philosophy are never determined at random. They have their origins in a historical necessity, not in the chance interests of a particular thinker. Philosophy aims at a complete rationality. But the rationality of our conclusions does not depend alone upon the correctness of our thinking. It depends even more upon the propriety of the questions with which we concern ourselves. The primary and the critical task is the discovery of the problem. If we ask the wrong question the logical correctness of our answer is of little consequence.

There is of necessity an interplay, in all human activities, between theory and practice. It is characteristic of Man that he solves his practical problems by taking thought; and all his theoretical activities have their origins, at least, in his practical requirements. That they also find their meaning and their significance in the practical field will command less general assent; yet it is, in my belief, the truth of the matter, and one of the major theses to be maintained here. Activities of ours which are purely theoretical, if this means that they have no reference to our practical life, must be purely imaginary — exercises of phantasy which are not even illusory unless we relate them to the practical world by a misplaced belief. The truth or falsity of the theoretical is to be found solely in its reference to the practical.

This may be what is intended by the assertion current in some philosophical circles that the meaning of a proposition is the method of its verification. If so, I can have no quarrel with this doctrine. I should like to be sure, however, that it is recognized that the method of verification with which the physical sciences have made us familiar is not the only way in which the theoretical can refer to the practical. There are other modes of verification; indeed, if there were not, the scientific mode would itself be invalid and indeed impossible. But this is not the moment to enter into these issues in detail. We must limit ourselves to what seems reasonable at a first inspection. For every inquiry must start from what is the case *prima facie*. We know how large a part of our thinking is concerned with the solution of practical issues. In such cases it is obvious to everyone that the reference is to practical behaviour, and that conclusions which have no bearing upon the solution of our practical problems are without significance. The theoretical question is posed by the practical situation; for that very reason the significance and the verification of the theoretical conclusion lie in the practical field. Indeed the theoretical result, if it is meaningful at all, is the solution of a *practical* problem. If then, as seems indubitable, all theoretical problems have their ultimate, if not their immediate, origin in our practical experience it seems reasonable to expect that all must find their ultimate meaning in a reference to the practical. It may indeed turn out otherwise. There may be generated, by the instigation of practical experience, a set of theoretical activities which have their meaning in themselves and require no practical reference to sustain or to validate them. But it would be a methodological error to assume this from the start.

This does not mean, however, that the reference of theoretical to practical activities is always direct or obvious. Nor does it mean that in our reflection we can or should always be aware of the practical reference. It does not justify a pragmatic theory of truth nor suggest that we should not seek knowledge for its own sake. The disinterested pursuit of the truth may be, and, I am convinced, is in fact, a condition of the practical efficacy of reflection. The inner life of the spirit is not merely technological: it is not condemned to a servitude to practical ends which are set for it without its knowledge or consent. The essential reference of theoretical to practical activities does not involve the control of theory by practice. It consists even more significantly in the control of practice by theory; in the determination, through reflection, of the ends of action. All that is contended for is this, that there is a necessary relation between our theory and our practice, that the activities of reflection can never be totally unrelated to practical life; that it is always legitimate to ask, of any theory which claims to be true, what practical difference it would make if we believed it. It may often be difficult to answer this question, but if the correct answer were that it would make no difference at all, then the theory would be a mere exercise of phantasy, neither true nor false, but meaningless.

I have laboured a truism because I am thinking primarily of philosophy. For here, if anywhere, it might seem to be true that we are involved in a theoretical activity which has no practical reference. This I am concerned to deny. In philosophy, indeed, the reference to practice is indirect and remote throughout much of its range. Here too it is especially important that the question of the ultimate reference to practice should not obsess the thinker, or control the processes of his reflection. But it is also in philosophy that the ultimate reference of theory to practice is most decisive and far-reaching. It is not for nothing that some have held that a philosophy is a way of life; or that common tradition conceives the philosopher as a man of a balanced temper, who meets fortune or disaster with equanimity. Our western philosophy began with the breakdown of a way of life in ancient Greece, which posed the question 'What should we do?' If it has found itself driven to dwell almost exclusively with the sister question 'How can we know?' it remains true that this question is incomplete in itself; and that the complete question, in the end, is 'How can we know what we should do?'

SAA 21–24

Macmurray did not share the mistrust of philosophical system-building which was rife among his contemporaries in English philosophy during the 1950s and 1960s.

The adequacy of a philosophy depends upon its range; upon the extent to which it succeeds in holding together the various aspects of human experience, and exhibiting their unity.

SAA 39

The misunderstanding, however, against which it is most important to guard, touches the purpose, or the philosophical function, of these lectures. Because they range, in a systematic fashion, over every general aspect of human experience, they may suggest that what is offered is a new philosophical system. This is not the case. Unlike many of my contemporaries, I have no objection to system-making; I consider it, indeed, in its proper place, a necessary part of the philosophical enterprise. Most systems of philosophy, indeed, are the product, not of the genius of the original thinkers to whom they are ascribed, but of the industry of their commentators. But there are system-builders among the great philosophers. Aristotle, Aquinas, Hegel are examples. Their function is to give a definitive and systematic expression to a process of thought which has been unfolding itself over a period of history. At the beginning of such processes stand the pioneers, thinkers like Pythagoras or Descartes, whose function it is to reject current presuppositions and to establish a new point of view, with new assumptions. The process itself, which unites these two extremes, consists in the gradual discovery of the implications and consequences of the new point of view. The present work is a pioneering venture. It seeks to establish a point of view. Its purpose, therefore, is formal and logical — to construct and to illustrate in application the form of the personal.

A new philosophical form cannot be established by demonstration. It can only be exhibited and illustrated in use. It is possible to show the need for new formal construction by a critical analysis of the philosophical tradition. The forms in actual use — at present the mechanical (or mathematical) form and the organic (or dialectical) — can be shown to prove inadequate to their function. The analysis can be used to indicate the *locus* of this inadequacy, and so to suggest the starting-point of a new construction. Further, the analysis of this starting-point can be made to yield the form which it implies and the presuppositions which this form carries with it. But the verification can only be undertaken through an attempt to apply the new form over the whole field which it must cover. The function of a philosophical form is to exhibit the unity of human experience as a whole, in all its general aspects, both theoretical and practical. To verify it is to show that it is capable of doing so. This explains the appearance of system-building. It has been necessary to consider each major field of human activity, both practical and reflective, in systematic order, from the new point of view, and to offer at least the suggestion of a theory in each which might be compatible with the new form. But this process has been carried only to the point where the application of the form has been sufficiently illustrated. What has been attempted is to indicate, in each field, the modification of traditional theory that seems to be required. The paramount interest has remained the same throughout — to clarify the form and to exhibit its philosophical adequacy.

SAA 12f

Modern philosophy begins with Descartes' famous assertion, 'I think, therefore I am.' Like many philosophers, Macmurray found this formula inadequate. Philosophy is by its nature theoretical, but he wanted to theorize from the standpoint of physical action rather than from that of private thought processes.

Speech is public. It is at once thought and action, or rather a unity of which 'mental' and 'physical' activity are distinguishable but inseparable aspects; and as a result it establishes communication, and introduces the 'you' as the correlative of the 'I.' For if the 'I think' logically excludes the second person, the 'I say' makes the second person a logical necessity. The 'I say' is logically incomplete. To complete it we must formulate it as follows: 'I say to you; and I await your response.' Thus the problem of the form of the personal emerges as the problem of the form of communication. Contemporary existentialism, which concerns itself with the matter of personal experience in its personal character, equally, and perhaps more consciously exhibits the emergence of the new problem. But here the problem shows a religious face. In the tension between its theistic and its atheist exponents it revolves around a religious axis, and formulates the problem of the personal in the antithesis: 'God — or Nothing.'

The final question, then, which the Critical philosophy leaves on our hands is this, 'Is it possible to take its conclusion — that reason is primarily practical — as the starting-point and centre of reference for a new effort of philosophical construction?' Can we substitute for the 'I think' the 'I do'? Kant insisted that we cannot. Is he justified in this? In the end the only answer must be to attempt it; the only refutation of Kant's negative must be to *do* it. For since the reason for Kant's denial lies in the acceptance of the 'Cogito' as his own centre of reference, it cannot be conclusive, and it may help us towards the effort we must make if we consider the 'Cogito' as it was originally formulated by Descartes, who established it as the starting-point of modern philosophy.

There is no need to consider any of the traditional criticisms of the Cartesian formula *'Cogito ergo sum.'* For the original assertion was intended to make a radical break with philosophical tradition and to establish a new starting-point. By its success it initiated a new philosophical tradition, and consequently all criticisms of it within the tradition which it established, are internal criticisms which depend upon its acceptance. They can only be criticisms of the manner of its formulation, not of what is formulated. The 'Cogito' establishes a new starting-point and centre of reference for philosophical reflection; it can only be challenged from outside the tradition it establishes, by establishing a different starting-point, with which it can be shown to be incompatible.

Historically, the 'Cogito' represents a challenge to authority and a declaration of independence; and so well did its author know this that he went in fear of the penalties that his boldness might incur. For Descartes it was equivalent to the assertion 'I am a substance whose essence is thinking.' If we eliminate the terms 'substance' and 'essence,' which would limit its application to the first period of modern philosophy — (the second period substitutes the assertion 'I am a thinking organism') — we may paraphrase its significance for its time in the following way. 'I am a thinking being: to think is my essential nature. I have therefore both the right and the duty to think for myself and to refuse to accept any authority other than my own reason as a guarantor of truth.' In this way the 'Cogito' constitutes an appeal from authority to reason.

SAA 74f

Macmurray also rejected Descartes' method of comprehensive doubt, since such doubt could not be genuine.

The method of doubt rests upon an assumption, which should be made explicit, that a reason is required for believing but none for doubting. The negative, however, must always be grounded in the positive; doubt is only possible through belief. If I find myself possessed of a certain belief, and know no reason for questioning it, I *cannot* doubt it; and if I could my doubt would be irrational. Moreover, if I do doubt one of my beliefs, then it is no longer a belief of mine, but only something that I used to believe.

It may be objected that this is to make an elementary mistake by confusing practical with theoretical doubt, and so failing to distinguish between logical certainty and psychological certitude. This is an internal objection, for the distinction itself derives from the method of doubt. In making the criticism we are indeed revealing the origin of the distinction between certainty and certitude, which is one aspect of the dualism of theoretical and practical which follows from the 'Cogito.' Since we are doubting — for good reasons — the adequacy of this standpoint, its implications have become problematical for us, and arguments which presuppose it are invalid. Belief and doubt are primarily practical; and from the standpoint of practical experience the distinction shows a different face. If in practice I believe, for instance, that I am surrounded by objects which have an independent material existence of their own, I can *pretend* to doubt this, without really doing so. If we call this a 'theoretical' doubt, we must beware lest the phrase misleads us into thinking that there are two species of doubt. A 'theoretical' doubt, in this usage, is an imaginary or non-existent doubt. When we talk about the lion and the unicorn we are not distinguishing two species of vertebrate animals. There are lions; there are no unicorns. We might agree to express the difference by calling unicorns 'theoretical' animals. But it would be foolish to conclude that there ought to be a science of 'theoretical' biology, and set out to explore systematically the rational structure of the world of theoretical organisms.

It cannot be true that I ought to doubt what in fact I believe, by a deliberate act of will. For this is an impossibility, and 'ought' implies 'can.' If then I am asked to adopt the method of systematic doubt, I am invited, as a matter of principle, to pretend to doubt what in fact I believe. What shall I gain by engaging in this game of make-believe? We are told that it is the proper way to start a systematic quest for the truth. In the end, it is hoped, we shall exchange our practical belief for a theoretical certainty. But what probability — I shall not ask what *certainty* — is there that this will be the result? Is it likely that a sustained effort of pretence will lead to knowledge? And if, by some happy chance, this theoretical certainty does emerge, what guarantee have I that it is not an imaginary certainty; and the knowledge which it certifies, a mere pretence of knowledge?

SAA 76f

In Macmurray's view, Descartes sent philosophy off in a direction which inevitably led to atheism. As Macmurray found atheism unacceptable, this was another reason for rejecting Descartes' starting-point.

This philosophical tendency to discount the possibility of a natural theology is confirmed by the most vigorous and challenging of contemporary developments in theology itself. The Theology of Crisis has stressed the complete otherness of God to a point where the notion that reason could even suggest the divine becomes evidently irrational, and the idea of a natural theology itself unnatural. So, in our time, philosophers and theologians tend to unite, it would seem, in agreement that religion must rest upon its own evidence, and that any knowledge we may have of the divine must be revealed to us in 'religious' experiences whose validity is evidenced by an inner conviction of their authenticity in those to whom they are granted.

When both philosophy and theology tend in this matter to recognize an impassable gulf between faith and reason, it would seem that the philosopher, who must stand by reason, should conclude to atheism. He cannot admit, as premises of his argument, any special experiences, religious or other, whose validity is at all questionable. He must start from common experience at its most universal and its most ordinary; and his procedure must be by rational analysis and rational inference. At no point can he admit as evidence any experience which is radically heterogeneous with this commonplace starting-point, and which could point to no evidence in common experience to bear witness for it. Such a disparity between normal and religious experience would convict of unreality the abnormality of the latter. If there is no point at which faith and reason can meet, then it is unreasonable to accept the deliverances of faith, and atheism is the reasonable conclusion.

It is undeniable that the historic development of modern philosophy has moved in this direction. In its beginnings it is unquestioningly theist, and confident of its capacity to demonstrate the existence of God. Even Hobbes and Machiavelli profess a religious belief which we should consider hardly compatible with their modes of thought. This early confidence has gradually faded; and in the end has been replaced by the conviction that any attempt to sustain religion by philosophical reasoning is to be suspected of special pleading. The long argument which Descartes initiated has moved decisively in the direction of atheism.

It may be said that this is only history, and that it merely reflects the progressive decline of the authority of religion in our civilization during the modern period. There is truth in this. Yet the history of our philosophy is our social history at its most serious, its most reflective and its most logical. May not the failure of reason to sustain the argument for religion be in turn part of the explanation of the decline of faith? I do not wish to argue these issues now. I shall content myself, at this stage, with expressing my belief that the more closely modern philosophy keeps to its programme, and the more purely objective its procedure becomes, the more inevitable is the atheism of its conclusion. Within the limits of its assumptions no other result is permissible.

SAA 18f

– 3 –

The unity of the personal

Macmurray's philosophical work culminated in the publication of his Gifford Lectures, The Form of the Personal, *in the two volumes* The Self as Agent *(1957) and* Persons in Relation *(1961). He believed that attempts to interpret human behaviour through mechanistic and organic metaphors were inadequate in conception and harmful in their effects. A new logical form was required to do justice to personal life. In his Gifford Lectures, Macmurray suggested what this form might be (see p.66), and applied it to all aspects of human experience in order to see how illuminating it proved.*

At the beginning of his Gifford Lectures Macmurray outlines the threat to personal life posed by a functionalist view of the individual's relation to the State.

I need hardly labour to convince you that the cultural crisis of our time is a crisis of the personal. This is too general a conclusion of those who look deeper into the troubles of our society than the superficial level of organizational strain, whether economic or political. I need only refer to two aspects of the situation, both very familiar, in order to make clear what I mean by a crisis of the personal. One of these is the tendency towards an apotheosis of the state; the other the decline of religion. The two are intimately connected; since both express a growing tendency to look for salvation to political rather than to religious authority. The increasing appeal to authority itself reflects a growing inability or unwillingness to assume personal responsibility. The apotheosis of political authority involves the subordination of the personal aspect of human life to its functional aspect. The major social revolutions of our time all wear this livery, whether they are fascist or communist in type. The justification offered by the democracies for resistance to the death against both is the same, that they rest upon a philosophy which sacrifices the personal values, and so the personal freedom of men to the exigencies of political and economic expediency. At this level, the crisis of the personal is the crisis of liberalism, which was an effort, however ambiguous, to subordinate the functional organization of society to the personal life of its members. Yet nothing could be more revealing of the depth of the crisis we are facing than one fact. Communism rests upon a criticism of liberal democracy. Liberalism, it maintains, contradicts itself. While it stands, in theory, for human freedom, in practice it is a defence of human exploitation. Communism set out to resolve this contradiction by abolishing exploitation and realizing freedom in social practice. The declared intention was to achieve a form of society in which the government of men would give place to the administration of things. Yet its own practice, we see, defeats its intention, and leads to an apotheosis of the State and to an organized and efficient exploitation of its citizens. In communist practice the personal is subordinated to the functional to a point at which the defence of the personal becomes itself a criminal activity.

The decline of religious influence and of religious practice in our civilization bears the same significance. Such a decline betrays, and in turn intensifies, a growing insensitiveness to the personal aspects of life, and a growing indifference to personal values. Christianity, in particular, is the exponent and the guardian of the personal, and the function of organized Christianity in our history has been to foster and maintain the personal life and to bear continuous witness, in symbol and doctrine, to the ultimacy of personal values. If this influence is removed or ceases to be effective, the awareness of personal issues will tend to be lost, in the pressure of functional preoccupations, by all except those who are by nature specially sensitive to them. The sense of personal dignity as well as of personal unworthiness will atrophy, with the decline in habits of self-examination. Ideals of sanctity or holiness will begin to seem incomprehensible or even comical. Success will tend to become the criterion of rightness, and there will spread through society a temper which is extraverted, pragmatic and merely objective, for which all problems are soluble by better organization. In such conditions the religious impulses of men will attach themselves to the persons who wield political power, and will invest them with a personal authority over the life of the community and of its members. The state is then compelled to perform the functions of a church (for which by its nature it is radically unfitted) and its efforts to do so will produce, the more rapidly the more whole-hearted they are, a crisis of the personal. If we remember that history has brought us to a point where we must think of human society as a whole, and not limit our outlook to the confines of our own nation, there must be few who will fail to recognize, whether they welcome it or recoil from it, that we are involved in such a crisis.

SAA 29–31

In one of his earliest books, Interpreting the Universe *(1933), Macmurray analysed the mechanistic and organic modes of thought, or 'unity-patterns,' as he termed them. The following extracts are all taken from* Interpreting the Universe. *They outline the features of these unity-patterns and demonstrate their failure as ways of understanding human personality.*

Now, the construction of a synthesis of elements depends upon the representation of unity. It implies the presence of an idea of structure through which isolated symbols can be bound together to form a whole. The representation of this idea of a whole is what we may call a schema or pattern of unity. Its function is to guide the activities of the imagination, in its efforts to combine symbols or ideas, in such a way that their combination shall produce such a map of reality or of some part or aspect of reality as will serve the purposes for which thought is undertaken.

In this chapter I wish to consider the most general and, therefore, the most abstract of the unity-patterns which thought employs. I refer to the mechanical unity-pattern of mathematical thought. Like all the principles of symbolic construction, this one is determined by the purpose which underlies it, and by the function which it serves in personal life. It arises from the necessity of manipulating physical objects and is, therefore, adapted to the representation of reality so far as reality is stuff to be used, or to put it more technically, so far as reality is material. The idea of matter is the idea of stuff, of raw material which is formed in accordance with our purposes by our action upon it. When, therefore, we represent the world as matter, we are representing it as the field in which we exercise constructive activity, as that which we use for productive purposes.

When we are interested in anything as material to be used,

we are not interested in it for its own sake. The value which it has for us is an economic value, that is to say a utility-value, a value which is derived entirely from the purpose for which the thing is to be used. But to use things we must understand them, within limits. We must understand what they can be used for, and this understanding depends upon a knowledge of those characteristics which make them usable for one purpose or another. Any characteristics which they possess that have no use-value we shall ignore. Now, the characteristics of anything which make it utilizable are its causal properties, and, therefore, the understanding of things from the point of view of their economic value will be limited to an understanding of their causal properties.

Suppose, then, that the reflection which lies at the basis of an activity of thought is caused by a failure in our use of things in an immediate practical activity. The thought that results will be concerned to represent and to interpret reality as matter, and so to understand reality as a set of causal properties which can, if properly understood, be utilized for practical purposes. There are two main points to notice here. The first is that in such thinking any individual thing will be symbolized not for its individuality but merely as a bearer of general properties. For when we wish to use anything we are concerned merely with the general characteristics which enable us to use it. If there are other objects possessing the same characteristics, they are all equally useful as instruments for our purpose, and any one of them will serve just as well as any other. It follows that in such a case the same symbol can be used to represent all objects which have the same general characteristics and, therefore, the same causal properties.

In the second place, things which are considered from the material point of view are considered in terms of what they can do. They are means to certain ends. When we cease acting and withdraw ourselves from the use of things, the conception of means and ends, which is a practical conception, gives place to the conception of cause and effect, because we have ceased to be agents. In reflection upon the world as matter, therefore, whatever we consider will appear as the cause of an effect or as the effect of a cause, and whether it appears as cause or as effect will be purely a question of the order in which it is taken relatively to other things. Everything from this point of view is either cause or effect as you please to take it. Further, since we are not really concerned with anything as this individual thing, but merely as a bearer of general properties, the understanding of its causality will be an understanding of its general causal properties. This means that what we are concerned to represent and understand are the general principles of causal relation. I say 'relation,' because the idea of using a thing commits us to considering it essentially in relation to something else, never in and for itself.

We have here, then, a type of reflection which is at once limited in its scope and yet of universal application. It is limited because it considers everything from a limited point of view. It is universal because everything in the world can be considered from this limited point of view. Everything, that is to say, is at least material, however much more it may be. Everything can be considered as potentially usable. What we have now to discover is the unity-pattern which is demanded as the basis of symbolic construction in this type of reflection.

ITU 85–88

The mechanical universe

Since whatever is represented through mathematical symbolism must have its activities referred beyond itself, it necessarily presupposes the existence of something which is not and cannot be represented in the symbolism. Any attempt to use mathematical thought as a final explanation of the nature of reality must inevitably be involved in an infinite regress. However far you cast your net, however much you include in your system of symbols, it will remain true that your representation refers you beyond itself to an external cause. A mechanical and deterministic interpretation of the universe, such as mathematical analysis imposes upon the mind, must, if it is taken as a final and complete explanation, be self-contradictory. For in claiming completeness it claims to include everything within it, while its form compels it to refer whatever it includes to something beyond it. It is involved both in asserting and in denying the existence of something beyond. If there is something beyond what it represents it is no longer complete; if there is nothing beyond it, what is represented must, as a whole, be self-determining in its activity and, therefore, not mechanical.

We can now answer the final question: 'What kind of interpretation of the universe will be provided by mathematical thought, and how far will it be adequate to the world as we know it?' We have to notice that all thought is mathematical in type if it uses as its basis of analysis the unity-pattern which we have described. It need not necessarily employ pure mathematics as its instrument, though it will be most accurate and reliable when it does. What is fundamental to mathematical thought is the analysis of the object into a set of unit-elements and their arrangement in an order. Such an analysis forces upon us, through the nature of the abstractions employed, a mechanical interpretation of action. It follows that any interpretation of the universe which is based upon this type of symbolic representation must represent the universe as a mechanism in which all action is completely determined in accordance with causal laws.

ITU 97f

The analysis of mathematical thought enables us to conclude that materialism must be false because it is inherently self-contradictory. It implies the universality of mechanistic determinism as an explanation of action. To account for an action mechanically is to account for it in terms of a force acting upon it from outside. To interpret the universe in mechanistic terms therefore, is to interpret it in terms of something beyond it which acts upon it. But by definition there can be nothing outside the universe to act upon it. Mathematical thought can only be applied to finite systems falling within a wider environment. Its presupposition is that there must be a source of energy outside the system which it analyses and seeks to understand. It cannot, therefore, be applicable to the universe as a whole. In other words, philosophical thought cannot be valid if it is mathematical in type.

We can see this more correctly if we return to the point from which we started. Mathematical thought, and therefore science, arises from a particular kind of concrete situation. It arises from our interest in using things, and applies only to things in so far as they are utilizable. That is why it issues in materialism. The conception of matter is the general conception of things as material or stuff. Clay, for example, is the material or stuff which the potter uses to make his pots. And it is called matter or stuff precisely because it is passive to the action which he exercises upon it. The universe as matter is the universe as stuff which is passive to action, and the very conception implies an agent or source of action outside it and acting upon it. Matter is essentially a relative conception. It is relative to an agent that uses it. There can, in the strict sense, be no such thing as a material cause, though there may be a material instrument. For 'matter' means that in which effects are produced, and 'cause' means that which produces effects. By definition, therefore, the conception of cause is inapplicable to matter. That which is cause is necessarily the agent, while matter is that which is the patient. The agent is that which acts; matter is that which is acted upon. Therefore, the conception of a universe which is material and nothing more can only arise through a misunderstanding. It would have to be a universe in which there was nothing to act, and in which, therefore, there was and could be no activity at all. The misunderstanding arises because we forget, as the process of thinking goes on, the abstraction with which we started. And we reach a materialistic and deterministic conclusion precisely because we started by limiting our thought to the consideration of that in the world which is mechanically determined.

This conclusion is very liable to be misunderstood. There is a deal of truth in Bergson's insistence that the function of the intellect is to deal with matter. The method of thought which is most familiar to us, and which we habitually employ, is mathematical in type. Our tendency, if we accept the conclusion, will be to vitiate it by interpreting it in terms of mathematical thought. We will tend to think that some things in the world are mechanically determined while others are not. The vicious dualism between matter and mind is itself the product of a mechanical analysis. *Everything* in the world is material. It may be that nothing in the world is merely material, though certainly much that is in the world is more nearly pure matter than the rest. Even in the field of what we usually call material objects, there seem to be features which escape from the meshes of the mathematical net. But organisms and persons, whatever more they may be, are certainly material objects. It follows that there is nothing in the world as we know it in immediate experience, to which mathematical thought is inapplicable. The proper way to state the limitation of this type of symbolic interpretation is to say that it is valid for reality *in so far as it is material*. It would be wrong to say that it is only valid for material objects. It is, in fact, valid for anything that can be acted upon, or anything that has a material aspect that can be used as an instrument or be the means to an end. But it is only valid of anything within this limit. So far as anything is more than passive, not merely a means or an instrument, it possesses characteristics which cannot be represented in this symbolism, and which, for that reason, cannot be dealt with by the activities of mathematical thought. The limits of mathematical thought are, in fact, the limits of science. Science cannot offer us and should not be expected to offer us an interpretation of the universe. It is limited by the abstraction which creates it, and to apply its results beyond these limits is merely to be unscientific and illogical.

ITU 99–102

The unity of living things

Let us consider first what is sometimes called the material basis of life, by which is meant the arrangement of the elements in a living creature so far as it is material. We should note in passing that this involves disregarding for the moment the essential fact that life is a process of development. We take the living creature at one moment, and consider it as it is at that moment. In fact, life never *is* at any moment. It is always *becoming*. We often talk as if the material of which a living body is composed were preserved throughout its life. Yet life is essentially, so far as it is material, a process of metabolism. It consists of getting rid of the material of which the body is composed, and replacing it continuously by new material, not exactly but with variations. The matter of the living body is not preserved. It is in a continual process of dissolution and replacement. The form is preserved, but again not exactly, but with variations.

If we abstract from its growth, and take a cross-section, as it were, of the life of the organism at a particular moment, we find that it consists of a set of parts or elements which differ from one another. These differences are so arranged that they preserve a form. This general characteristic dictates the first characteristic of the unity-pattern that reflection requires. We must represent the unity of what is alive as a unity of differences, not as a unity of identities. It follows that the organic whole cannot be represented as the sum of its parts. You cannot sum differences. How, then, can the unity of differences be represented?

It can be represented only in aesthetic terms, as a balance or harmony. The work of a painter, for example, consists, in part at least, in combining different colours harmoniously so that they can produce an effect of unity. A work of art is always a unity of differences and that is why we often speak of it as an *organic* unity. Such a unity is felt, not calculated. It may seem that this is a drawback from the point of view of reflective thought. It is, in fact, only a drawback from the standpoint of mathematical thought, or from the standpoint of the logical intellect which wishes to perform its tricks in isolation from the other capacities of consciousness. Life itself is apprehended in immediate experience only through a co-operation of sense and feeling. We need not be surprised to find that the reflective representation of life involves the co-operation of feeling for harmony, rhythm and balance, with the ordinary processes of intellectual activity. Apart from this, the representation of life in symbolic form is just impossible.

The living thing, then, must be represented as a harmony of differences to form a unity. This, however, ignores the essential processes of growth. These must also be represented, if we are to think of life at all. This can be achieved by representing the different elements in the unity as themselves in process, and these processes of the different elements as themselves harmoniously combined to form a unity of processes which is the life of the organism as a whole. Each of these processes which are elements in the life-process of the individual organism will be represented as a function of the whole process. We shall say that each different element in the living creature has a function to perform in the whole, for the whole. We shall recognize that the differences of the material elements in the organism are determined by and relative to the differences in the function which each has to perform in the life of the organism. Form, we shall say, is relative to function, and the unity of the organism is a unity of functions.

There is still a third element which demands representation in the unity-pattern before it can be complete. It is the fact of development. It would be quite possible to imagine a unity of functions which should be purely cyclical, in which a cycle of interrelated activities repeated itself mechanically *ad infinitum*. But life, as we know it, is not merely this. It involves development in time as well as the repetition of processes. It involves this not merely relatively, within the life of the individual, but also absolutely, in the development of species, which is nothing but the extension of growth beyond the life of individual organisms through the processes of reproduction. Growth can perhaps be defined as reproduction with variation, even within the life of the individual, but that is a point which we need not consider here.

If we consider any finite process of development we notice that it has to be completed before we can apprehend it as a whole. Its beginning does not reveal its full nature. We do not know the nature of a seed until we know the full grown plant from which it is derived and into which it will itself develop. To understand a process of development it is necessary to know its final state, or at least its state of complete development. Earlier stages are only stages in the process because they lead to a mature state. An organism can be defined only in terms of its maturity, and its growth only as the series of forms which it takes on in its progress to maturity. For this reason the representation of life must be teleological. The life of an organism can only be described and understood by reference to the final state of its natural development.

ITU 108–12

... we may consider whether the organic unity-pattern can properly be used as the basis of a philosophical interpretation of the universe. Perhaps the simplest way of stating this question is to ask, 'Is the universe an organic whole?' Modern idealism answers this question in the affirmative. But in doing so it is apt to offer the organic type of interpretation as a substitute for thought of the mathematical type and so to misuse the organic unity-pattern. In doing so it claims implicitly, and sometimes explicitly, to supersede mathematical thought and science. The difficulty which then faces it is this, that if the universe is an organism there can be no organisms in it, for the different elements in the organic unity-pattern cannot themselves be organic wholes. They must be merely differentiated functions of the organic whole. The whole is either not an individual at all, or else the only individual. On the other hand, a modern realism — like the philosophy of Professor Alexander, for example — does involve a true understanding of the way in which the unity-pattern of biological thought can be applied to the interpretation of the world. It represents the mathematical structure of the universe as falling within and providing the basis for its structure as an evolutionary development.

But now, even if it is properly applied, the organic form including the mechanical form within it, the unity-pattern is inadequate to represent the universe as we know it in immediate experience. In the first place we have to notice the limitation of teleology. Its use depends upon the representation of a stage at which growth is complete, and unless this stage is represented the process of life cannot be defined. The earlier stages are all relative to the stage of maturity. Now, our immediate apprehension of life is the apprehension of the infinity of life in finite individuals and, therefore, the process of life is *known* as an infinite process, that is to say, as a process which has no final stage. It follows from this that it is impossible to represent the unity of the world which is given in immediate experience in terms of the organic unity-pattern. Just as in the case of mechanical thought, this type of symbolism must be limited to the interpretation of the finite. It can represent the final life-processes of individual organisms or of species or even of the whole process of evolution up to date, provided that we take the appearance of rational consciousness in humanity as the final stage. Beyond this it cannot go, and yet in its very nature it demands that all stages shall be represented as transitions to a more highly developed stage.

In the second place, the conception of the finite organism is meaningless except in relation to the conception of its environment. Here is another point in which we find the demand for something beyond the organism, in terms of which it can be an organism. The moment we begin to apply the unity-pattern to the world as we know it, we discover that we cannot understand the living creature in terms of itself. Its life, and hence its growth, though it is essential to its own nature, though it is, that is to say, an inner spontaneity and not the effect of an impressed force, is nevertheless conditioned by its environment and proceeds as an adaptation to the environment and as a response to the stimulus which the environment alone can provide. It follows once again that such a symbolism cannot be applied to the universe as a whole, since, if it were, the universe would need an environment to provide the stimulus to which its evolution could be the response. And the universe, by definition, can have no environment.

We see, then, that the effort to represent the universe as an organic whole must fail. The symbolism is inherently inadequate to the purpose for which it is used. Philosophical thought cannot be successful if it bases itself upon the unity-pattern of biological thought, however accurately it understands and applies its symbolism. The concrete point in our immediate experience of the world, at which the difficulty is brought into clear focus, is our experience of human personality. It may be possible to re-present subjective and irrational forms of consciousness in terms of the biological unity-pattern. But it is certainly not possible to represent the nature of rational or objective consciousness as we know it in immediate experience, through this form of symbolism. Human consciousness is not organic. When we return to consider this aspect of our immediate experience of the world, we discover the need for another and more adequate form of symbolism to describe and express what we know.

ITU 118–21

How are we to represent the type of unity which we know in our experience of the personal? A person cannot be represented as a mathematical unit because, though each person can say of himself 'I am I,' no person can say of any other 'I am I' or 'I am you,' but only 'you are you and not I.' And apart from this difference of I and you, there would be neither the one nor the other. The units of material existence are bare identities. One unit is identical with every other and its equivalent. Thus, two mathematical units have no real otherness between them. In the case of two persons, both are individuals, yet their otherness is essential to their individuality. For each of us, there can be only one 'I.' The other person is always 'you.' Yet it is equally essential to my being that in knowing you I know that for yourself you are 'I' and for you I am the other, the 'you.' This can obviously not be represented by mathematical thought, for which all units are equally 'it.' The difference between I and you must be represented in any symbolism which is to be of use in formulating our experience of the personal.

Organic thought, as we saw, does involve the representation of the essential differences between elements in the whole. But this expression of difference is in terms of complementary functions so that no element in an organic whole can be really individual. Only the whole can possess true individuality. For this reason organic thought, in its turn, cannot express the nature of the personal. For the personal involves the essential

individuality of all persons as well as their differences. Two
persons in personal relation are not complementary. They do not
lose their individuality to become functional elements in an
individuality which includes them both. In fact, in the personal
field the only real individuals are individual persons. Groups of
persons are not individuals. Nevertheless, the individuality of a
person exists only in and through his relationship to other
persons and the more objective his relations become with other
persons, the more his individuality is enhanced. It would seem,
therefore, that the unity-pattern of psychological thought must
somehow succeed in combining the characteristics both of
organic and of mathematical thought. It must express at once the
independent reality of the individual and the fact that this
individuality is constituted by the relationship in which he
stands to other independent persons who are different individuals. To put it in the familiar terms of modern controversy,
mathematical relations are external to the terms they relate.
Organic relations are internal to their terms. But personal
relations are at once internal and external. They create not
merely a unity between individuals, but also the difference of
the individual, which they unite. Further than this we are not in
a position to go. Any further advance would involve the solution of the problem which is emerging in our own time as the
central problem of contemporary philosophy.

ITU 138–41

Towards the end of Interpreting the Universe, *Macmurray says that
a logical form has to be found which can do justice to the nature of a
personal Self. In his Gifford Lectures he presented the form as follows.*

The unity of the Self is neither a material nor an organic, but a
personal unity. The logical form of such a unity is one which
represents a necessary unity of positive and negative modes. The
Self is constituted by its capacity for self-negation. It must be
represented as a positive which necessarily contains its own
negative.

SAA 98

*A logical form is necessarily abstract, and the only way to appreciate
the value of Macmurray's conception is to study the two volumes of*

The Form of the Personal, *in which it is applied systematically and illuminatingly to the whole range of human activities. We can note here that this formula allows for the personal experience of inner division and struggle, and for the habitual element in human behaviour, without which personal intentions could not be realized in action.*

We must notice, in the next place, that the material and the organic levels of reality are included within the personal. The full existence of a person includes a material and an organic existence. Indeed, it might be more illuminating to point out that the idea of the organic and of the material are, in fact, limitations within our personal consciousness. We do not build up our conception of the personal from our knowledge of the material world. On the contrary, we reach the conception of matter by leaving out certain aspects of our personal experience which we consider to be peculiar to our personal and organic existence. The importance of this consideration is that it indicates that a personal conception of the world includes the organic or the material conception of it. Here again the persistent dualism between mind and matter dogs our footsteps. To assert that the world is spiritual is not to deny that it is material. In a properly personal conception of the world there is no denial of materialism. On the other hand, to assert materialism as the last word about reality is to deny its personal character and, indeed, its organic character.

RE 223

– 4 –

The nature of reason

Macmurray was happy to agree with the ancient view that reason is what differentiates human beings from the animal kingdom. He did not, however, identify reason solely with the capacity for intellectual analysis and speculation. Both the intellect and the emotions could be either rational or irrational. Reason, as Macmurray defines it, is our capacity for objectivity.

We associate reason with a state of mind which is cold, detached and unemotional. When our emotions are stirred we feel that reason is left behind and we enter another world — more colourful, more full of warmth and delight, but also more dangerous. If we become egocentric, if we forget that we are parts of one small part of the development of human life, we shall be apt to imagine that this has always been so and always must be so; that reason is just thinking; that emotion is just feeling; and that these two aspects of our life are in the eternal nature of things distinct and opposite; very apt to come into conflict and requiring to be kept sternly apart. We shall even be in danger of slipping back into a way of thinking from which we had begun to emerge; of thinking that emotion belongs to the animal nature in us, and reason to the divine; that our emotions are unruly and fleshly, the source of evil and disaster, while reason belongs to the divine essence of the thinking mind which raises us above the level of the brutes into communion with the eternal.

RE 16

If we are to discover the nature of emotional reason we must first be sure about what we mean by reason in general. It is, in the first place, that which distinguishes us from the world of organic life; which makes us men and women — super-organic. It is the characteristic of personal life. This, however, is only a formal statement. We want to know what are the particular ways in which reason reveals itself in human behaviour. One of the most obvious is the power of speech. Another is the capacity to invent and use tools. Another is the power to organize social life. Behind all these there lies the capacity to make a choice of purposes and to discover and apply the means of realizing our chosen ends. We might go on to draw up a list of such peculiarly personal activities; though it would probably not reveal immediately the root from which they all spring. There are, however, certain persistent cultural expressions of human life which are in a special sense characteristic of our rational nature at its best. These are science, art, and religion. This calls attention to one point at least which is highly significant. Whatever is a characteristic and essential expression of human nature must be an expression of reason. We must recognize, then, that if we wish to discover what reason is we must examine religion and art just as much as science. A conception of reason which is applicable to science but not to religion or art must be a false conception, or at least an inadequate one. Now the obvious difference between science on the one hand and art and religion on the other is that science is intellectual while art and religion are peculiarly bound up with the emotional side of human life. They are not primarily intellectual. This at once forces us to conclude that there must be an emotional expression of reason as well as an intellectual one. Thinking is obviously not the only capacity which is characteristically human and personal.

The definition of reason which seems to me most satisfactory is this. Reason is the capacity to behave consciously in terms of the nature of what is not ourselves. We can express this briefly by saying that reason is the capacity to behave in terms of the nature of the object, that is to say, to behave objectively. Reason is thus our capacity for objectivity. When we wish to determine why anything behaves as it does, we normally assume that it behaves in terms of its own nature. This means that we need only find out how it is constituted to understand why it responds to a particular stimulus in a particular way. We are apt to make the same assumption when we are considering how human beings behave. When we do this we are met by a special difficulty which is usually discussed as the difficulty about the freedom of the will. The controversy about free will is insoluble, not because the facts referred to are irreconcilable, but because the problem itself is wrongly conceived. We are looking for something in the inner constitution of the human being to explain the peculiar nature of his behaviour. We are still assuming that he must necessarily behave in terms of his own nature, like anything else. It is precisely this assumption that is at fault. Reason is the capacity to behave, not in terms of our own nature, but in terms of our knowledge of the nature of the world outside.

RE 18–20

Reason is traditionally the *differentia* of the human. If the personal individual is essentially the thinker, then rationality must refer to the logical faculty, and to this faculty in contrast with the empirical capacities which belong to our practical nature, and even to the empirical processes which provide data for a psychological account of thinking. Rationality becomes the capacity to draw correct conclusions from premises; and we postulate that as rational beings this capacity belongs to all of us and is identical in all. This, I say, is a specialization of the term rationality. But to say this is to say too little. For if we use the term in this sense, while at the same time we use it to denote the *differentia* of the human — that which distinguishes us from the brutes — we are in error. The human *differentia* we have decided is not the capacity to think, but the capacity to act. If, then, we continue to use the term 'rationality' in the specialized theoretical reference we must surrender its use to denote the essential characteristic of the personal. If, on the other hand, we prefer to retain its use as defining the human or personal field as distinct from the non-human, we must give up the specialized reference to logical thought. Reason becomes, then, the capacity to act, and only in a secondary and derivative sense the capacity to think, that is to say, to pursue a merely theoretical intention. It seems to me that there is good reason for choosing this latter course, since choose we must, or abandon the term 'reason' and its derivatives altogether. For the use of reason to denote the *differentia* of man is the more fundamental and the more stable.

PR 26

– 5 –

The self

Since the time of Descartes, philosophical thought about the nature of the Self has tended to conceive this entity — if indeed it has been granted the status of an entity — as isolated and purely mental. But if reason is the capacity for objectivity (see previous Chapter), a rational Self must be related, through bodily existence and physical action, to other Selves and to a material environment.

The Self must be conceived, not theoretically as subject, but practically, as agent. Secondly, human behaviour is comprehensible only in terms of a dynamic social reference; the isolated, purely individual self is a fiction. In philosophy this means, as we shall see, that the unity of the personal cannot be thought as the form of an individual self, but only through the mutuality of personal relationship. In face of both difficulties a radical modification of our philosophical tradition is demanded. The first requires us to substitute for the Self as subject, which is the starting-point of modern philosophy, the Self as agent; and to make this substitution is to reject the traditional distinction between the subjective and the objective. The second compels us to abandon the traditional individualism or egocentricity of our philosophy. We must introduce the second person as the necessary correlative of the first, and do our thinking not from the standpoint of the 'I' alone, but of the 'you and I.'

SAA 38

... The adoption of the 'I think' as the centre of reference and starting-point of his [Kant's] philosophy makes it formally impossible to do justice to religious experience. For thought is inherently private; and any philosophy which takes its stand on the primacy of thought, which defines the Self as the Thinker, is committed formally to an extreme logical individualism. It is necessarily egocentric.

SAA 71

The Self conceived as 'spectator of all time and all existence' itself becomes a mere idea, since it is excluded from participation in what it contemplates. There is no place for it in the world. And whatever world its vision may be conceived to apprehend consists of its own ideas, as Descartes rightly recognized. It is more illuminating to recognize it frankly as solipsism; and to accept this solipsism for what it is — a *reductio ad absurdum* of the theoretical standpoint. Existence cannot be proved; it is not a predicate. Yet the isolated self — the thinker — must prove existence if he is to apprehend the Other. The given for reflection is always idea — whether it be concept or image, and not less if it be that end-product of the analysis of sensory experience which is now entitled 'sense-datum.' We know existence by participating in existence. This participation is action. When we expend energy to realize an intention we meet a resistance which both supports and limits us, and know that we exist and that the Other exists, and that our existence depends upon the existence of the Other. Existence then is the primary datum. But this existence is not my own existence as an isolated self. If it were, then the existence of any Other would have to be proved, and it could not be proved. What is given is the existence of a world in which we participate — which sustains and in sustaining limits our wills.

Since then the Self as Subject is the isolated Self, we can transform our earlier conclusion that the Self exists only as Agent. We may say instead that the Self exists only in dynamic relation with the Other. This assertion provides the starting-point of our present argument. The thesis we have to expound and to sustain is that the Self is constituted by its relation to the Other; that it has its being in its relationship; and that this relationship is necessarily personal. Our main effort, therefore, must be directed towards determining the formal characters of personal relationship.

PR 17

– 6 –

Action and habit

Macmurray's conception of the Self as an agent was fully outlined in the Gifford Lectures, but he was developing the idea in his earlier writings. He distinguished human action from mechanical events and organic development. True action is consciously intentional.

Now, the idea of reality, and therefore the distinction between real and unreal belongs to the level of intentional activity. To speak quite strictly, nothing can be *done* without an intention. Action is inherently intentional. Where there is no intention there are only events which happen. When a person does something unintentionally we call the change that is produced accidental. Accidents happen in the course of our action; they are not integral parts of it. We are not directly responsible for them. If we are held responsible, it is on the ground that if we had been more careful they would not have happened. We have therefore to draw a distinction between actions and events; a distinction which we can mark clearly by saying that events happen, while actions are performed.

Events are not performed and actions do not happen. Whenever we conceive anything as an event, we imply that it is not an action. In other words, all events are matters of fact; while no actions are matters of fact, but matters of intention. The world of fact consists of things and events. Things are, as it were, the static components of the world of fact, and events the dynamic components. What characterizes this world of fact is the absence of intention and, hence, of action. This distinction between fact and intention is the basis of all practical consciousness. From the point of view of any person who is acting deliberately in the world, his environment is not mere fact. It appears rather as a set of possibilities which limit the intentions which he can realize in action. What, from a purely passive point of view, is mere fact, is, from a practical point of view,

something that can be acted upon, and so altered or used in
some way or other. The knowledge which is the cognitive
element in a practical activity is knowledge of what is possible.

BS 206f

We come back finally to the necessity of a knowledge of action
which is not and cannot be scientific, because it must be intrinsic
and not instrumental. We need a knowledge which will enable
us to act rightly. On such a question, scientific psychology can
have nothing to say, since the question is no longer a question
of fact but a question of intention. It will not be denied, I think,
that the knowledge of how we can control our behaviour for the
achievement of intentions presupposes the existence of intentions which we may attempt to achieve. What may be denied is
that there can be any knowledge in this field. We may represent
our intentions as being fixed and unalterable, and all questions
as to which intentions are right and which are wrong as
inherently meaningless. This is the view which is ordinarily
expressed — and by no means well-expressed — when people
say that values are subjective, or that they are matters of taste.
If this were so, there could be no knowledge of value. The only
knowledge possible would be scientific in type, confined to
matters of fact. This knowledge would still be instrumental,
since it would enable us to achieve our intentions; and the
existence of the intentions would make it possible to describe
the actions undertaken to realize them as right or wrong. In that
case the rightness of the act would lie in the fact that it did
achieve its intention.

This view seems to me still to involve a confusion between a
motive and an intention, between matter of intention and matter
of fact. It implies that an intention is a subjective fact. If it were,
an intention would not be an intention but a motive, and the
distinction between right and wrong, even in the limited sense,
would be impossible. It is not difficult to see that an intention is
not a subjective fact. It is true that when I intend something my
intending it is a subjective fact; but *what* I intend is a change in
the objective world, and it is this future change in the objective
field that is the intention of my action. It is obviously wrong to
describe a future change in the objective world as a subjective
fact. But it is also wrong to describe it as a fact at all. This can
be seen most easily in the case where an action fails to realize its
intention. In that case the future change in the objective world,

which was the intention of the act, is not realized and never becomes fact at all; yet this does not imply that the action had no intention. The intention of an action is not then matter of fact. It is not an event in the mind which can function as the cause or motive of a movement of the body which in turn can cause other changes in the objective field.

BS 253–55

Human action is intentional activity. The activities of human beings, when they are not intentional, lack the essential mark of humanness. We recognize this in our feeling that a person is not responsible for what he has done unintentionally. Intentional activity, as the phrase suggests, is the unity of two moments, an ideal moment which we call an intention, and a material moment which we call an activity. These two moments must not be looked upon as two distinct things or events which are joined together. The intention is not the cause of the activity, or the activity the effect of the intention. An intentional activity is, in fact, a single unit of human behaviour. It is what we refer to as an action. But it has these two moments, or aspects, of thought and activity combined in it, and in reflection we can abstract the one from the other. It is also true, however, that we can separate them, though only by ceasing to act intentionally. We do this when we stop to think. In thinking our intention does not go so far as action. We remain, as it were, shut up in our own minds. So far as we live a life of reflection and contemplation, our life becomes a life in the mind, with knowledge or feeling as its end and aim. Now obviously this cannot mean that our material activities come to an end. It can only mean that our intentionality has been withdrawn from them, so that they go on, in some sense, 'of themselves' as matters of habit and routine. When we turn from reflection to action, what happens is not that our minds become blank while our bodies exercise themselves. It is simply that the conscious intention which characterizes us as human beings is shifted to the outside world. Whereas in reflection we are engaged quite literally in changing our minds, in action we are engaged in changing the world. Action includes thought; it is not something which can be distinguished from thought. The life of reflection is not a different life from the life of action. It is a limitation of the life of action to one of its aspects. This is why we contrast ideas and real things. This is why ideas are true or real only through their reference to reality, and not in their own right. Reality is only to be found in action. Real things are the things we deal with in action, and therefore the whole life of thought has meaning only in reference to the full reality of intentional action upon the world which includes it. Now, it is possible for us to limit our intentional activity in this fashion to what we call the life of the mind. But we can only do so by refraining from carrying our intention beyond ideas into action, and by allowing action to be determined automatically. The life of action then ceases to be specifically human. This negation of action is under certain circumstances necessary and justifiable, but only so far as the withdrawal into the world of ideas is itself subordinated to an intention which looks beyond it to a return to intentional action. It is only when the world of thought is related to the world of action as means to end, and the intention in thought is to use its results in action that thought is significant. The reality of thought always consists in its reference beyond itself.

CH 6–8

In Macmurray's later analysis of action we see what might be termed an existentialist element, emphasizing the uncertainty and irrevocable choice involved in any action performed.

Now let us turn to another implication of action, which we can best formulate in the proposition that *action is choice.* Consider again our solitary agent in empty space. He is aware of space as the possibility of moving in an infinite number of directions from his present position. But if he moves, it must be in one of these directions and in no other. He cannot move in several directions at once. Now since action is irreversible, when he acts, and so moves in one of the possible directions, all the others become, by his action, impossible. His action, then, is a choice of one possibility which negates the possibility of all the others. They become past possibilities, which are no longer actually possible. To do anything is to do *this and not that.* After it is done I may wish I had done something else, but I cannot do it. What I have done remains actual and I cannot undo it. Action is thus the actualizing of a possibility, and as such it is choice. It is important to notice that this means precisely what it says. It does not mean that an action is preceded by a choice; nor that a mysterious 'act of will' somehow connects a theoretical selection with a physical movement. This is only an attempt to construe the mystery of action from a dualist point of view. There may indeed, in particular cases, be a reflective activity which precedes action, and which consists in deciding, between a number of alternative courses, which is the right course to pursue. But this is only a theoretical, not an actual choosing; as is shown by the fact that the action so 'chosen' may not in fact be performed. The actual choice is the doing of the action; and action is choice whether or not this preliminary reflection takes place. There can, undoubtedly, be no choosing apart from reflection; but this need only be that primary reflection which is in action, as one of its dimensions.

That action is choice discloses another implication of action which it is important to clarify. The distinction between right and wrong is inherent in the nature of action. Knowingly to actualize one of a number of possibles, and in doing so to negate the others, is to characterize the act that is so performed as right and the others as wrong. Again, it is the doing of the action which so distinguishes between right and wrong, not a theoretical judgment which may or may not precede, accompany or follow the doing. Consequently, if we may say that a proposition is that which can be true or false, we may also say that an action is what can be right or wrong. The question which underlies any philosophical inquiry into action is, 'How can I do what is right?' It is not, 'How can we know what it is right to do?' If this second question were to prove unanswerable, it would not follow that the first question was so too. The belief that we can only do what is right by first knowing what it is right to do and then doing this is an assumption. It implies the very principle which Kant was so rightly concerned to deny, that the good can be determined as an object in time. For it presupposes in ourselves two capacities to neither of which we can lay claim — theoretical infallibility and practical omnipotence. If I am to do what is right by first deciding what it is right to do in the circumstances in which I must act, my moral judgment must be infallible. If not, I may be mistaken, and if I then do what I judge mistakenly to be right, not merely have I done wrong, but I could not have done otherwise. But this is not all. Suppose we grant to ourselves this infallibility of moral judgment, what follows? I know absolutely, before I act, what I ought to do. If I then seek to do it, I may fail. Circumstances over which I have no control may intervene, and I discover, in the event, that what I have done is not what I set out to do. Again I have not done what is right; and again I could not have done it. Whatever may be true of our ability to judge what is right — and can we really believe that it is not liable to error? — it is certainly untrue that we have an absolute power to carry out our decisions and achieve our objectives. In some sense, 'ought' implies 'can.' In some sense, therefore, if we can act rightly, it must be without a prior theoretical determination of what it is right to do. The discrimination of right and wrong in action must be prior to and not dependent upon the theoretical discrimination of the truth or falsity of a judgment.

                                                                    SAA 139–41

An action, if it is not to be mere activity, requires an element of reflection. Reflection is of value only in so far as it leads to renewed and more effective action.

The succession of positive and negative phases, of movement and of reflection, is so characteristic of the personal life that it would be well to have a name for it. We shall refer to it whenever we meet it as 'the rhythm of withdrawal and return.'

In most practical activities, the withdrawal into reflection is forced upon us because we meet unforeseen difficulties. We have to stop what we are doing and consider the next step. It may be that alternative procedures present themselves, between which we must choose, and the relative advantages and disadvantages of these must be considered. It may be that the means we are using fail to produce the expected result; and we have to think out a new method of procedure and start afresh. In all such cases the periods we spend in reflection and consideration fall within a dominant practical purpose, and are negative moments in the realization of a practical intention. We may notice here that the relative time spent in action and in reflection is of no theoretical importance. Many actions involve little reflection and much practical activity; others require much careful planning and then perhaps a single decisive act. Many would have been accomplished more speedily and more successfully if longer time had been spent in considering each step in advance.

We have been considering activities in which a definite and fairly clearly defined end is in view. But many of our activities are not of this kind. Others consist in exploiting such means of action as we possess. These originate rather in a consideration of our resources and the possible activities in which they may be employed. In such cases the ends are, in a sense, dictated by the means. But the important point in this is that just as the same end may be attained by various means, so the same means may serve the attainment of various ends. Because of this it is possible to accumulate power — that is, the means of attaining our ends — without deciding in advance between the alternative purposes to which the power shall be put when we have got it. The accumulation of wealth is a case in point, since the richer I am the more alternative possibilities of action I possess. In such activity, the ultimate end remains undefined, and the intention terminates in the means, over long periods of time in many cases. Indeed, since the use of the power which is being accumulated may be postponed indefinitely, the pursuit of power may become, for a particular agent, an end in itself, however irrational and even meaningless such an intention may be. For power of any sort has meaning only in reference to an end beyond itself to which it is the means.

The intention here is still practical. But clearly it need not be. The reflective moment in a practical activity is itself concerned with the means to the realization of a practical end; and in many cases the knowledge it achieves can be applied in different activities than the one for which it was originally intended. Knowledge indeed is power in a special sense, and any increase in knowledge is an increase in power; since knowledge is actually a dimension of action, and without it an increase in material resources is nugatory. Consequently, the generalization of knowledge, as the negative aspect of action, makes possible an activity which intends the accumulation of knowledge, without any defined reference to the practical intentions which it makes possible; and so without reference to its application in action. The moment of withdrawal into reflection may be prolonged indefinitely, and the operative intention will then be a theoretical intention, with no specific reference to any practical intention to which it is the means. So knowledge may become an end in itself; even though this too is irrational and meaningless. For in the absence of all reference to the practical reflection becomes phantastic, incapable of either truth or falsity.

This then is one way in which it can be shown that though when we start from the primacy of the theoretical we can find no way to the possibility of action, yet when we start from the

'I do,' the possibility of reflection is no mystery; and the dualism
of mind and matter is overcome.

SAA 181–83

If we concentrate on what happens habitually we develop the idea of
laws of human behaviour. But in doing so we may ignore those aspects
of behaviour which make us conscious agents.

The laws of which we have been speaking are particular laws;
but what is usually meant by a law of Nature is general. These
general laws of Nature are derived from the particular laws by
generalization. From the formula for a particular frictionless
pendulum we can derive a formula for all frictionless pendu-
lums. For in all cases, though some elements vary, others remain
constant. If this were not so they could not be instances of the
oscillation of a pendulum. The formulae of the different instances then will exhibit constant elements and variable elements. We can therefore devise a general formula in which the
constant elements provide the determinate structure and the
variables are represented by special symbols. This is our general
law, which can be applied, in any particular case, by determining the value of the variables for that case. In other words the
law of a particular instance can be derived from the general law,
by determining what is variable in it. The general law holds for
all instances of a class. If we ask, then, what makes them all
instances of a class, the answer will be that the general law
applies to them all. If this seems to beg the question — and in
a sense it does — we must refer to what has already been said
about classification. Clearly before we can determine a general
law, we must have a principle of classification which is independent of it. But this principle need only be *prima facie*: it may
require modification as our knowledge progresses. Observed
resemblances may provide a rough starting-point: but in view of
what has already been said about the secondary character of the
'observational' point of view, it would be at least more fundamental to say that we begin by classifying together all instances
in relation to which we find in practice that we can act successfully in the same fashion. The original constants are to be found
in our own modes of action, for which, of course, perceptual
resemblances are an original, if somewhat untrustworthy guide.

A 'law of Nature,' then, is a pattern of continuance, and the discovery of such 'laws' is the discovery of such patterns in our experience of the Other. To say of any group of phenomena that it obeys a law is to assert that it contains a pattern of change which recurs without change. To say that Nature in general obeys laws, or that all phenomena occur in accordance with laws, is to assert that Nature is the Continuant, or the non-agent in temporal existence.

SAA 156f

In the personal field this organic continuance appears as habitual activity. Our habits are those elements in our practical activity which are recurrent responses to recurrent stimuli. They differ from instinctive reactions only in the fact that they have to be learned in the first instance, and consequently can, in principle, be unlearned. Normally our habits are continuously qualified by the intentional action within which they fall and which they make possible. All actions depend upon a system of habitual responses to stimuli; and the formation of habits is the necessary basis of every action. If we cross a busy street, we concentrate our attention upon our objective and upon traffic to be avoided, and determine the direction, the changes of direction and the timing of our movements. The rest — and it is the greater part — of our activity is automatically adapted to these conscious determinations. Here habit is clearly the negative aspect of our action, without which the action could not take place. It is integrated with and subservient to the positive aspect of deliberate purpose in terms of which the action must be defined. This can be clearly seen by contrast with abnormal cases in which a habit becomes compulsive, and escapes from deliberate control. Only then do we find an activity which is *purely* habitual, and for which the agent is not immediately responsible.

Such an autonomous habit is a behaviour pattern which recurs without change. It follows that if we can determine the pattern, we can formulate a law which will enable us to predict the future behaviour of the agent in respect of every recurrence of the particular stimulus to which the habit is a response. Now suppose that this particular autonomous habit is common to a group of persons, or to all persons. Then the law of the habit could be generalized, and the behaviour of all agents in the group could in this respect be predicted. Suppose then that we proceed as psychologists, in precisely the same way as the physicist does, by abstracting from action and considering only that aspect of personal behaviour which is constituted by habit. We can then study the activities of persons *as if they were purely continuant*. We can make experiments with normal persons who will agree to behave in accordance with our instructions, and not for their own ends and on their own initiative. In this way we can isolate, under laboratory conditions, those aspects of human behaviour which would normally be habitual responses within deliberate action. Alternatively, we may study abnormal individuals, suffering from neurotic or psychotic diseases, and so observe actual cases of behaviour which is isolated from normal control by the agent. On the basis of such systematic observation we may seek to determine psychological laws of human behaviour in a thoroughly scientific fashion, and verify them in the usual way. The knowledge that we obtain can be used, just as in the case of physics or biology, for the deliberate control of human behaviour.

SAA 161f

Motive and intention

We must consider for a moment at this point the conception of 'motive' in action, and in particular its distinction from and its relation to 'intention.' The distinction between motive and intention is difficult, and indeed impossible, for any philosophy which accepts the primacy of the theoretical, and takes its stand upon the 'Cogito.' For the motives of our actions are not thought, but felt; and if we represent them as thought, they become indistinguishable from intentions. From the standpoint of the Agent, however, the distinction is both important and clearcut. One aspect of the difference, from which we may begin, is that the motive of an action need not be conscious, while the intention must be. To talk of an unconscious motive makes sense; but 'an unconscious intention' is a contradiction in terms. The phrase could only signify 'an intention which is unintentional.' An action, in the sense in which we are using the term, is necessarily intentional. It is indeed the presence of intention which distinguishes it from activities which are non-rational, uninformed by knowledge. Now we have already found that if we abstract from the element of knowledge which constitutes action, we are left with a motive consciousness, whether at the level of feeling or of sense; and also that this motive consciousness, or rather this conscious behaviour falls within action as a negative aspect. Every action, then, has a motive. But it does not follow that the motive determines the action, or that the agent is conscious of his motive; or if he is somehow aware of it, that he attends to it. What determines an action is its intention; but we shall be prepared to find that the motive of an action is contained within the intention as its negative aspect.

The term 'motive' signifies, in general, that which determines movement. Its scientific equivalent is 'energy.' But its characteristic use is limited to directed movements; to movements which have a purposive character. In organic behaviour, therefore, motive is that which accounts for the release of potential energy in response to a stimulus. Where we suppose consciousness to be involved — say, as a feeling of fear — then this feeling is the motive of the reaction, since it accounts for the direction in which energy is expended in movement. Because the reaction is defensive, that is to say, an avoidance of danger, we require a motive to account for its purposive character. But we do not suppose, or at least we have no reason to suppose, that any cognition is involved. The organism does not *know* that it is in danger, or what the danger is. Consequently its response to stimulus has a motive, but no intention; and this motive awareness accounts for the reaction, and determines its character.

In the case of agents, however, motives do not determine action. Nevertheless, all action contains necessarily an element of reaction to stimulus, without which it would be impossible. We call this habit; and the system of habits in an individual agent we call his character. The reason, we have seen, for distinguishing personal habits from organic responses to stimuli, is that they are not innate but have to be learned. They are formed in action, and they are subject to deliberate modification and reformation. But once formed, and while they persist, they operate through an automatic or semi-automatic response to recurrent stimuli; though this is always complicated by the presence of cognition. In so far then as an agent acts habitually, he acts from a motive, but not with intention. But in normal action these motived responses are aspects of an activity which *is* intentional; and because attention is concentrated upon the objective, the motives of these habitual aspects of action normally remain unconscious, unless they are brought into consciousness by reflection.

In all conscious behaviour then, the motive is a feeling, which governs the expenditure of energy by selecting its direction. This control includes the negative phase — the inhibition of movement. The basic differentiation of feeling is into positive and negative forms, which determine movements of attraction and of repulsion respectively. We must therefore distinguish between positive and negative motivation; the positive controlling the activities which constitute the life-process of an organism, the negative being defensive. Feeling, we have seen, is differentiated both quantitatively and qualitatively, and its distinguishable modes are combined in very complex patterns; each of which is more or less positive or negative according to the preponderance of positive or negative elements in it. Sensory consciousness, when it is present, rests upon and is itself controlled by feeling, which directs energy to the formation of images; and these images in turn modify feeling. Mere sensation, unassociated with feeling, is an impossibility; and if it were possible it could not of itself determine a reaction. The function of sensation in activity is to make possible a wider range and a finer discrimination of possible reactions, in particular by anticipation. But the selection of the direction of response remains the function of feeling.

Now in personal activity, all this organic activity falls within action, and is therefore raised to the level of intention. With the distinction between Self and Other, both images and feelings are referred to the Other, and action is determined by knowledge. This knowledge has two aspects, a determination of the Other as matter of fact in relation to action and so an apprehension of the possibilities open to the Agent; and a valuation of these possibilities in action, and so the determination of an intention. These two aspects of knowledge are of course not separable in fact, but only distinguishable by thought. The discrimination of the Other — as support for and resistance to action — is perception; the valuation of alternatives is matter of feeling.

When we refer to the motive of an action, in distinction from its intention, what we have in mind is the constellation of feeling in which it originates. Any state of feeling has a tendency to express itself in action; and would do so unless controlled by intention. Under abnormal conditions we do find instances of behaviour which escape from intentional control and are completely determined by their motives. When a person loses his temper, or is overwhelmed by passion or falls into a panic this is what happens. Then, as we say, a man 'becomes irresponsible,' or 'loses his self-control,' or 'acts purely on impulse.' In such circumstances the distinction between motive and intention is particularly clear. We must not forget, however, that the patterns of feeling which constitute our motives are themselves the product of an intentional experience; and that they continue responses to the environment which have been deliberately established in the past. The impulsive activities of an agent are therefore normally 'in character'; though they are not determined by a present intention. A person's character is the persistent system of motives from which he acts under normal conditions; and when we predict what he is likely to do in given conditions from a knowledge of his character, we abstract from intention, and suppose that his motives will determine his actions. Motive, we may then say, is the continuant element in action; it determines the general direction of an agent's behaviour, while the particular actions he performs are determined by the particular intentions he forms from moment to moment in terms of his discrimination and valuation of his situation as he knows it. Nor is there any reason, in principle, why he should not act intentionally in complete opposition to his momentary inclination; for inclination is simply the tendency for feeling to realize itself in action, which is normally subject to intentional control.

SAA 194–98

– 7 –

Knowledge, belief and verification

Macmurray's long-term practice of science explains the value he placed on action and experiment as means of gaining knowledge. In his contributions to the symposium Adventure *(1927), he anticipated the importance of an idea later to be developed by Sir Karl Popper: that scientists gain knowledge not through attempting to verify their ideas, but through trying to falsify them.*

Science starts not from facts but from beliefs. The belief-basis is originally instinctive, but long before we reach any deliberate search for knowledge it has been elaborated into a system by the natural functioning of the mind and by the pressure of experience. In our own day, for example, the belief from which the scientist starts is the whole body of systematic theory which forms the accepted content of his science. It is this that he criticizes by experiment.

Now his experiment compels him to treat this 'belief' as hypothetical only. His business is to test its truth in a particular case. To the scientific mind, therefore, no theory is ever final or absolute. It is always subject to revision, and it cannot be revised by mere thinking. The belief itself is a system of orderly thought, and for that very reason thinking in terms of the belief must fail to revise it. Thought cannot lift itself by its own waistband. A belief can only be revised by acting upon it, and deliberate action is only possible upon the basis of a belief. This is the point which is central to our subject. The scientific attitude and method is an effort to amend beliefs by accepting them as a basis for experiment. We might say, with pardonable exaggeration, that the scientist experiments with his knowledge, not in order to prove it true, but in the hope of proving it faulty. Many of the great advances in the history of scientific thought are the result of experiments which turned out contrary to expectation.

The critical moments in the progress of knowledge are usually those at which a logical demonstration is shown by experiment to be faulty, in spite of its logical correctness.

A 34f

The idea of the 'verification principle' became widely known through A.J. Ayer's 1936 book Language, Truth and Logic, *in which he popularized the ideas of the 'Vienna Circle' of scientists and philosophers. Macmurray had heard a member of the Circle, Moritz Schlick, speak in London some years before Ayer's book was published. As a scientist himself he sympathized with Schlick's emphasis on verification, but he did not share what he considered to be the narrow view of its nature later promulgated by Ayer and other 'logical positivists.'*

The issue now turns upon the nature of verification. For we must grant, it seems, that any assertion which requires verification, yet does not admit of verification, is meaningless; and any assertion which is reasonably doubted requires verification. From the standpoint which we have adopted, the weakness of the positivist case lies in a misunderstanding of verification; a misunderstanding which is inevitable if theoretical activity is taken to be self-contained and self-sufficient. On this presupposition verification must take the form of a reference from one aspect of reflective experience to another; that is to say, to sense perception. But a reference to sense-perception *as such* — that is to say, as a pure receptivity of the mind — verifies nothing. It only seems to do so on the assumption that what is given in sense-perception exists independently in its own right. We have already characterized the realist assertion that this is the case as a mere dogma. But it is a groundless assertion only upon his own presuppositions. If sense-perception is taken as an element in action, and not in reflection, the case is different. For then the reference in verification is not to sense-perception, but to action, in which, of course, sense-perception is a constitutive element; and verification is itself the testing of theory in action.

Now it follows from this that the field of verification is much wider than is commonly allowed. For in principle, wherever a reflective construction can enter into the determination of an intention it can be verified. What is required is simply an expectation in action which can be falsified in the event. What is expected may, of course, be a certain perceptual experience.

But clearly it need not be. A reflective valuation, as we have noticed already, can equally be verified in action. Then why not a metaphysical assertion? To say that it is meaningless could only signify that whether it was believed or not could make no difference to the intentionality of an agent. There may be assertions of this kind, though I cannot think of any which could be taken seriously. If there are such assertions, then I, for one, will happily agree that they are meaningless. But most meta-physical assertions, at least those which have been seriously maintained, are not of this kind. They are assertions which, if seriously believed, make a profound difference to the direction of human intentions. The differential consequences of the kinds of action which they promote constitute their verification. For to act upon a belief involves expectations which may or may not be falsified in the event. What is expected may not be a particu-lar sensory experience. Indeed if the belief is a metaphysical one it clearly cannot be. It must be remembered that even in science to verify a hypothesis does not mean to demonstrate its truth. No hypothesis can ever be established beyond the possibility of revision. What verification does is to provide practical grounds for believing an assertion, in preference to any known alterna-tive. Belief is a practical category; to justify a belief is to provide rational grounds for acting on the assumption that it is true. Since we cannot pursue the question how metaphysical beliefs are tested in action, I shall add only one further remark. If we can understand, to whatever extent, what difference would be made in our inention if we acted in the belief that a certain proposition were true, then that proposition has a meaning: and if the meaning of a proposition is its verification, in some sense of this obscure phrase, then the mode of verification to which it is susceptible is a clue to its interpretation.

SAA 215–17

The form of religious reflection is necessarily determined by its data; and these are our practical experiences of our relations with one another. How then do we know one another, and what form does this knowledge take? Clearly, it has a very different form from our knowledge of the material world. It is not, and cannot be, objective or scientific. A purely objective attitude to another person precludes a personal knowledge, because it excludes direct personal relationship. We can know a great deal about other people, both in particular and in general, without knowing them. The reason for this is simply the mutuality of the personal. If I know you, then it follows logically that you know me. If you do not know me, then necessarily I do not know you. To know another person we must be in communication with him, and communication is a two-way process. To be in communication is to have something in common. Knowledge of other people is simply the negative or reflective aspect of our personal relations with them.

From this there follows an interesting corollary. All knowledge of persons is by revelation. My knowledge of you depends not merely on what I do, but upon what you do; and if you refuse to reveal yourself to me, I cannot know you, however much I may wish to do so. If in your relations with me, you consistently 'put on an act' or 'play a role,' you hide yourself from me. I can never know you as you really are. In that case, generalization from the observed facts will be positively misleading. This puts the scientific form of knowledge out of court in this field. For scientific method is based on the assumption that things are what they appear to be; that their behaviour necessarily expresses their nature. But a being who can pretend to be what he is not, to think what he does not think, and to feel what he does not feel, cannot be known by generalization from his observed behaviour, but only as he genuinely reveals himself.

PR 169

For thinkers such as Ayer the verification principle rendered all talk of God strictly meaningless. Macmurray, while accepting the validity of such a principle, believed that the existence of God could be verified in human beliefs and their practical consequences. Like the existentialists, though, he saw that testing a belief in practice could involve a degree of commitment which might lead a person to risk their very life.

Perhaps the fundamental component of a belief in God is the expression in action of an attitude of faith or trust. Its opposite is an attitude of fear. A man who is on the defensive in his attitude to life does not believe in God, whatever his professions may be. Belief in God necessarily delivers a man from fear and from self-centredness, because it *is* his consciousness that he is not responsible for himself nor for the world in which he lives. It involves the recognition that his own life is a small, yet an essential part of the history of mankind, and that the life of mankind is a small but essential part of the universe to which it belongs. It involves the recognition that the control and the determination of all that happens in the world lies in the hands of a power that is irresistible and yet friendly. It is more than the recognition of this; it is the capacity to live as if this were so. It is the habit of living in the light of this faith. This is not all that is contained in the belief in God, but it is a fundamental and necessary element in it. Anyone who does not live as if this were the truth does not believe in God. Anyone who does behave in this way believes in God at least so far, whatever he himself may say about it.

CS 20f

... belief in God, whatever else it may involve, at least includes the capacity to live as part of the whole of things in a world which is unified. If we believe in God we live as if the fortunes of the world did not depend on us; we live as if the world could be trusted to work out its own destiny and to use us, even through our mistakes and our failures, for its own good purposes.

CS 22

From the standpoint of the agent, which is the presupposition of our whole argument, the question whether the world is personal is the question whether God exists; or rather it is the form into which the latter question must be translated. To ask, 'Does God exist?' implies the primacy of the theoretical. For it presupposes an idea of God which arises independently of a knowledge of His existence, and enquires whether this idea refers to any existent object. The problem so formulated is insoluble, for the reason that Kant advanced, that 'existence' is not a predicate. In reflection we are in a world of ideas — of images and symbols — and there is no way out. We can move only from one idea to another idea, never to an existing entity. But in action existence is given — as an existing self in relation with an existing Other. There is then no question of proving existence, but only of determining its character. This determination is by means of ideas which refer to it. The knowledge that the Other exists together with me is certain; but so soon as I go farther, as I must, and determine, in idea, what the Other is and what I am and how we are related, knowledge becomes problematical. The general question that arises is whether representation of what exists is adequate or inadequate. This adequacy refers to action, in which we are in existence; and the resolution of the problematic lies in the function of knowledge, that it makes possible, if it is adequate, the full realization of our capacity to act, that is, our freedom. Apart from our knowledge of existence in action, which is the mere zero of knowledge, our reflective knowledge is hypothetical and requires to be verified in action; and in action it may prove inadequate to what is required of it. This is the case whether it be perceptual or conceptual, whether it be knowledge of fact or of value, or knowledge of the personal Other.

Consequently, the theological question is improperly represented in the form 'Does God exist?' It must be expressed in the form, 'Is what exists personal?' More adequately stated this might run, 'Is the universal Other, from which the community of persons distinguishes itself, and which is the same for all persons, a personal or an impersonal Other?' More simply, if we distinguish ourselves — that is, all finite personal individuals whatever — from the world, we have to ask whether the world is personal or impersonal. We must remember, however, that this is a real question only if it has a reference to action. If it made no difference to action it would be meaningless — a merely speculative metaphysical conundrum. It would be incapable of any verification. But clearly we can live in the world in a fashion that is grounded either in a belief that the world is personal or that it is impersonal; and these two ways of life will be different. Consequently, the verification of the belief in God must lie in their difference; and in particular in the difference between the realization of freedom in the one and in the other.

PR 214f

All judgments of value, it is sometimes said, are simply emotive. They express merely our feelings, and cannot therefore be true or false. Only judgments of fact can constitute knowledge, since only these have an objective meaning which permits of verification. To this I must reply that such doctrine is itself a valuation and a false valuation at that. It expresses an exclusive overvaluation of intellectual reflection. That all valuation is the work of feeling I agree, and that its expression is an expression of feeling I have no doubt. But why 'merely'? Might I not as well say that an assertion of fact is 'merely' an expression of a thought that occurred in me? That logical thought is objective, while feeling is 'purely' subjective, is surely a dogma for which no rational ground can be offered. If our feelings are subjective because they occur in us, why not our thoughts which as surely occur to us? If our thoughts are objective because they refer to objects, then our feelings, which refer to objects in their own fashion, are objective also. If our thoughts are verified in action, so are our valuations. Is it not the case that our judgment that some experience which we seek will satisfy us is often falsified by the event? Both our feelings and our thoughts have their symbolic expressions; an assertion of fact which I make is an expression of my thought just as an assertion of value is an expression of my feeling. If it can be also a correct or incorrect description of an object, why may not the expression of my feeling for an object be a correct or an incorrect valuation of the object? And if an expression of feeling is emotive in the sense that it is an attempt to make other people feel as I do, is not the expression of what I think, in precisely the same sense, an effort to make other people think as I do? No relevant difference between the two modes of reflection is to be found unless it be this, that to verify a valuation I must commit myself in action by making it my end. Sometimes, indeed, I must stake my happiness, my reputation or even my life on the experiment; and if I find I was mistaken there may be no possibility of trying again.

SAA 202

– 8 –

Science: its scope and limits

Although Macmurray valued scientific activity, he believed that the kind of knowledge given by science is incomplete. Its methods can be applied to any area of life, but they reveal only a limited aspect of the subject-matter investigated.

Scientists are concerned to discover the regular, repeated patterns of behaviour in whatever is the subject-matter of their investigation. When such patterns are recognized, this knowledge can then be used as a means of achieving particular results in particular circumstances, and the way is open for the technologist to give it practical application. For Macmurray, the danger of seeing scientific knowledge as the model for all forms of knowledge was that such an outlook emphasized an instrumentalist approach to the natural world and humanity, and devalued artistic and ethical considerations.

In the first place, then, science concerns itself only with matter of fact. It excludes the determination of value. This refers only to the objectives of a science. Scientific activity, just because it is a human activity, is involved in valuation. To do is to choose; and to choose is to determine, as between alternative courses of action, which is the better. To be a scientist, after all, is to assert and to live by the value of knowledge, and of the sort of knowledge which science provides. Moreover, one cannot simply be a scientist; one must choose between one or other of the sciences. One must, for instance, either be a geologist or a botanist. And in the pursuit of one's chosen science one is continually faced with alternative procedures between which choice is necessary. But this involvement in valuation is not an objective but a postulate of science, and something which is inseparable from any activity; and the special valuations, if there are any, which are peculiar to science, are assumed or presupposed. They are not investigated. There is no science whose business it is to investigate and justify the presuppositions on which science in general, or any of the special sciences, is grounded. Such an investigation would be, not scientific, but philosophical; and indeed the investigation of scientific method has long been a recognized department of philosophical enquiry.

With this possible ambiguity removed, it is clear that science is concerned only with matter of fact, with what actually happens. This already excludes all preoccupation with value, and the determination of value, and so sets a limit for science. If it is allowed — as I believe it should be — that there can be knowledge of value, we could distinguish this sphere of knowledge from knowledge of fact, and assign the latter to science.

The second major characteristic of scientific knowledge is its generality. The search for valid generalizations is of the essence of scientific enquiry. The part played by observation and, in modern times, by description, in scientific research has been exaggerated. It used to be said, and in some quarters it still is said, that science begins by observing facts, and that out of the facts, when they have been collected, a theory to explain them emerges. To this it has been added that such theory is a generalized description of the facts on which it is based. Now in most sciences in their early stages, there is a good deal of observation and even of description, in the ordinary sense of these terms; but these activities are not specially characteristic of science. We shall have occasion to notice later on the part played by the exact observation and description of nature in some of the arts — in poetry and in painting particularly. It would be more accurate to say that science starts with a theory and proceeds to test its validity, when possible by experiment, and always by reference to accepted facts. There is a simple reason for this. Observation, if it is to be scientifically effective, must be systematic and selective. Only a theory — a working hypothesis will do — can guide research. We must know what facts to look for; and they are facts which will confirm or, preferably, invalidate a hypothesis. I say 'preferably' because confirmation leaves us largely where we were; it is by the discovery of the limitations of theory and its amendment, that science progresses. It is what turns out contrary to expectation that is the critical guide to the scientific imagination. Theory supplies the expectation.

As for observation, it has long ceased, in the basic sciences at least, to be a straightforward use of the senses in natural surroundings. It takes place in laboratories; and there the objects of observation are pointer-readings which record in some way the measurable results of highly artificial and contrived events; events which never would happen in the ordinary course of nature at all. It is doubtful, too, whether the end-product of this experimentation is properly called a 'description,' even a generalized one. In physics, at least, we reach points at which we are warned against using 'models' to describe the meaning of theory, and where we must be content, we are told, with the mathematical formulae which have been devised.

From this critical excursus let us return to what I called the 'generality' of science. The scientist is not interested in particular things, or particular happenings. He must, of course, deal with particulars, since any object or any happening is particular. Yet when he observes anything he thinks it as an instance of a kind. He abstracts from its particularity, and attends only to what it has in common with all other members of its class. This is not peculiar to the scientist: we all do it continually; and it will be important at a later stage to notice when and why we do it. But it *is* peculiar to science that it never does anything else. It is only concerned with the general, never with the particular in its particularity; as, for instance, the historian is. Perhaps the best way to express the aim of science is to say that it is the search for *constants;* that is to say, for patterns which repeat without change indefinitely. The patterns are, in particular, patterns of change and the formulae in which they are expressed become, when they have been accepted after validation, laws of nature. One should add, for completeness' sake, that a pattern of change may repeat with modifications, provided that the modifications take place according to a known pattern; as, for instance, in the case of gravitational acceleration.

This concentration of science on what is general or, at the limit, universal, is itself an exclusion, as any concentration of interest must be. Like the exclusion of value from the objective of enquiry it sets its own limit to science. Science is limited to the general, to that which is constant, to that which repeats itself indefinitely. It provides no knowledge of the particular, for the reason that it ignores particularity. The discovery of new facts, by the invention of new methods and new instruments of observation, is, of course, an important part of scientific progress. Many of these extensions of our capacity for observing reveal much that is fascinating in its particularity: but not for science.

The scientist, of course, since he is not merely a scientist, may share the enjoyment of this aspect of his discoveries. But for science itself these new facts have their place only as instances, and only as such do they have any bearing upon the advance of general theory.

At this point it may be useful to turn our attention to the origin of science in the normal non-reflective activities of daily life. Every mode of reflection has its origin here. All of them carry out systematically and persistently something that we all do spasmodically and uncritically as part of the practical business of living. We all ask philosophical questions, because we find ourselves in situations which force them upon our attention. We all have artistic experiences and artistic impulses; and religious tendencies are perhaps the most universal of all. But for all that we are not artists or philosophers, nor even persistently religious. For this it is necessary to devote oneself, systematically and of set purpose, to the development of one's natural capacities for this or that type of specialized activity, to undergo the requisite disciplines, to master what has already been accomplished by others in the selected field. Both in the arts and in the sciences, the activities in which they consist are carried on either necessarily, or most effectively, by specialists who have been designated for the task by natural gifts and technical training. One need not agree with the dictum that a specialist is a man who doesn't know anything else to recognize that a specialist activity is, of its very nature, a limited activity.

What then is the general field of practical activity in which the sciences have their origin? It must be a field which has the same characters that we have found in science itself. It must be a field in which we are not concerned with what should be done, with the ends at which we should aim; for a systematic effort to provide a basis for such decisions would be directly concerned with valuation, and science, we have seen, is not. Equally, it must be a field in which we are concerned with things not in their particularity but in terms of their general characters; in things of a kind, so that any one of the kind is as good as another. This is clearly the field in which we are concerned with things as instruments for our purposes. For in such situations our ends are fixed, and our attention is concentrated upon the means for their achievement. We are concerned, not with what to do, but with how to do it. Our problems are technical: they are problems of construction, for example, of transport, of the use of power. The resources for answering them lie in the world outside us, in the materials which nature provides. For such purposes, in general, we want to know what materials are available for our use, what their natural properties are, how they will behave under varying circumstances, and so forth. We must know the answers to these questions if we are to use our material resources satisfactorily. For other necessary purposes we need to know how plants and animals behave. For we have to grow crops, and rear, as well as hunt, animals. Such knowledge is amassed, in the first instance, by trial and error; and successful methods are built into social tradition as customary techniques. Under appropriate conditions, however, the effort to improve old techniques and invent new ones may become widespread, and then the time is ripe for the development of science as we know it — a mode of reflection which provides the basis for the development of technology.

In relating science, in this intimate fashion, to technical experience and to technology, I must not be understood to mean that the scientist is concerned with the solution of practical problems or with the applications of his scientific discoveries. It is not necessary that he should be, and oftener than not he is totally oblivious to them. It might be better, for science as well as for society, if he were less single-minded in his pursuit of knowledge for its own sake. I have never understood why people should think that scientific research should be more likely to be successful if scientists are blind to the practical importance of their work. The early protagonists of scientific studies, like Bacon, were well aware that the new kind of knowledge promised benefits for mankind which the traditional scholasticism could never offer; and this was one of the main grounds they had for supporting it. In our own day it is as surely the practical benefits and powers which science has conferred which have won it the central and privileged position which it occupies among us. But all this is beside the point. The motives and the objectives of scientists do not determine the character of scientific knowledge. What is decisive is the kind of questions which it investigates, and, even more, the kind of methods it employs. Scientific knowledge is instrumental knowledge; it is the kind of knowledge which provides the basis of technological advance. If I am asked for further evidence that the actual connection between science and technology is a necessary one, and in no sense accidental or adventitious, I shall reply by referring to the place assigned in science to experiment. I have suggested that a satisfactory account of scientific activity must represent it as proceeding by the testing of theory by reference to observed fact. It would have been preferable perhaps to say by means of experiment. It is customary to think of experiment as an appeal to sense-perception. It is, in fact, an appeal to action. To experiment is to do something practical on the basis of a theory and in doing it to anticipate the result. Its formula is, 'If this theory is correct, then if I do "X" I shall produce "Y".' What is this but an appeal to the technological efficiency of the theory as evidence of its correctness? Once I am satisfied of the correctness of the theory, then the experiment becomes a technological rule. If now I want to produce 'Y' for practical purposes, then I do 'X.' The experiment becomes a technique merely by a change of attitude, an alteration of the objective. As an experiment, the production of 'Y' is a test of the theory; as a technique it is the end-product of a process. This shows that any method of knowledge which validates theory by experiment necessarily produces the kind of knowledge which is a basis for technology. And this fact determines its limits as well as confirming its origin in the technical activities of everyday life.

We must consider the limits of science, finally, by reference to the attitude of mind which is requisite for the doing of it. The term which has become popular to indicate this attitude is 'objectivity.' The term has a long and honourable history as a technical term in philosophy, during the course of which its meaning has changed more than once. Now that it has come into common use it has become so ambiguous that it is difficult to employ it in any useful analysis. 'Objective' has come to be used even as a synonym for 'true'; but more commonly (and less absurdly) as a synonym for 'scientific.' It will serve us better, therefore, if we select certain essential elements in the scientific attitude of mind for notice, which are nowadays more vaguely covered by the term 'objectivity.'

The first essential component in the scientific attitude is an interest in the external world for its own sake. An older expression for this would be 'a disinterested desire for the truth.' This use of the term 'disinterested' to refer to a particular way of being interested is instructive. It betrays an assumption that all interest is self-interest; that all our interests are for our own satisfaction. If this were true, then all forms of reflection, including science, would be impossible, or at best, illusory. The point is of the first importance, since it is the basis of reason. If we could not, in some sense, escape from the circle of our self-satisfaction; unless we could have the centre of our interest outside ourselves, we could never be rational beings. To recognize something which affects our modes of experiencing — our capacity for sensing, for instance — as existing in its own right, independently of us and our experiencing, itself implies and depends upon our ability to be interested in it as an existent. This is the fundamental element in the concept of 'objectivity.' But this term, quite apart from the ambiguity which now affects it, has always, in its careful use, been limited to the activities of the intellect. It will be part of my contention that this limitation is a mistake; that activities of ours other than the intellectual share this characteristic, and in particular, that all our activities of reflection are rooted in it. For in reflecting, we are concerned to manipulate ideas, meanings and symbols; and to refer all this, which happens in us, to a world which is beyond and outside us. If we could not make this reference and carry on our reflection in terms of it, then all of it would be reduced to an activity of phantasy, without a meaning. We need, therefore, a term which indicates this human capacity of which 'objectivity' in the philosophical sense is a particular case. I propose to refer to it as our capacity for self-transcendence.

The scientific attitude of mind then, like all reflective attitudes, is self-transcending. What distinguishes it from the others is its impersonality. The scientist takes great care to exclude what he calls 'the personal factor' from his work. This does not merely mean that he allows for observational and other errors which may creep into the work of any fallible individual. It means even more the exclusion of the prejudices and desires, the hopes and fears, which are inseparable from the personal activity of any human being. He is, in fact, concerned to find in his work only the expression of what is common to all men; that his 'observer' should be an impersonal observer — that is to say, any observer so far as he is a pure observer — with all psychological elements excluded from influence upon the result which would differentiate him from any other. Thus on the subject side as well as the object side science demands a limitation to the universal aspect of experience, and the exclusion of individuality.

RAS 11–18

Technology and its power

It is clear ... that the proper limit of the application of science is the technical field. We assume that our objectives have been determined, that the standards to be achieved and maintained are recognized. There remains the problem of how to do what has been decided. It is this field to which the results of scientific reflection are properly limited. It is, obviously, an extremely large field, for technique is an element in all action; and over a wide field of activity the ends of human action are dictated by necessity. Limits are set to it by practical possibility, for there is much that is beyond the reach of human action. Science itself, however, is not so limited. The scope of our knowledge is far wider than the range of our practical control; and in principle there is nothing in the whole range of natural existence which is beyond the possibility of scientific investigation, and relatively little which is excluded by moral or other standards. The limits of application which interest us are, however, those set not by possibility but by propriety. These belong to the range of things which we can, but should not, treat as instruments of our purposes. We are, in particular, interested in the improper use of the extension of the technical powers which we owe to scientific reflection.

We live, we are told, in a scientific age. What does this mean? Clearly not an age in which a great deal of scientific research is being done, however true this may be. Certainly not an age in which scientific knowledge is widespread. The number of people who could pass a simple examination on any science is relatively very small. What is meant seems to be that in our time the effort to use science systematically for human purposes is characteristic. We look now to science for the solution of our social problems, as men once looked to religion. In other words, our characteristic social activity is the use of a progressive technology based upon scientific research. We might go further and say that a scientific age is an age whose major social end is the development and application of scientific technology.

Now technology of any kind is by nature instrumental. It is a means of achieving some end. The distinction between means and end can be applied as a principle of analysis to all action, though the application is neither as easy nor as simple as might be expected. The end is that for the sake of which the action is done. Consequently it dictates the means — the instruments and techniques which are employed. If then technology becomes an end, there has been an inversion of means and end. What is by nature means has become end. How is this possible? How is it possible that power, which is the general conception of means, should become an end in itself?

Two answers suggest themselves. First, many kinds of power are generalized means. They can serve many different ends. In a civilized society money is the clearest example. Consequently, it is possible to amass such means without deciding in advance the particular ends which they will be used to serve. And once a man has set himself in this fashion to amass power, the habit of life which he establishes may prove very difficult to break. The time for using his means may never arrive. Secondly, the desire for security may provide a strong motive to collect generalized power. In particular, the possession of power, quite apart from its use, can provide social prestige and social influence, and so security in relation to other people. In both cases power, in spite of being a means to ends in its natural character, can become an end in itself. Nevertheless, the inversion of means and ends in this fashion is always irrational, and finally ineffective.

Now in any society in which science is dominant, in which the scientific form of reflection has a higher prestige amongst the majority of people than either religion or the arts, one could expect to find that power is the effective end of social action. There are two main reasons for this which we must consider shortly in closing this lecture. The first concerns the continuous increase of technical capacity which science creates. The other is the type of mentality which the admiration of science encourages. In both cases science is actually determining social standards and social ends, and is operating out of bounds.

Scientific knowledge, we have seen, is instrumental. It makes possible the development of technology, and so the increase of power in society. This is matter of fact; and the recognition of this fact is the major reason for the increase in the social prestige of science. A scientific age is an age in which there is a widespread awareness of the increase in power made possible by science. The consequent valuation of science above other forms of reflective activity is evidence that the desire for the increase in power through the development of technology is a mainspring of social effort. The outstanding character of social action will then be the exploitation of power.

Consider what this means. To exploit power is to do something because it is possible, not because one has a good reason for doing it. The systematic exploitation of a continuously expanding technological capacity means that as new possibilities of action arise, we use them because we now have them, and not for any good to be attained by their use. The use of the new power has become a new value in itself. Means has become end. The fact that something has become possible is accepted as a reason for doing it. We have gone farther along this road than we realize; partly because it is always possible to disguise it as fulfilling, in each particular case, a real human need, partly because we have become so used to it that we take its value and its necessity for granted. Fifty years ago travel was very fast at 70 miles an hour. Today we fly from London to New York in seven hours. Technological improvements have already made speeds of over 1,000 miles an hour possible. So plans are already on hand to build passenger planes which will cross the Atlantic in two hours. We take it for granted that such planes will be operating a few years from now. No one asks what advantage humanity is to gain from this, or whether indeed there may be positive disadvantages which outweigh any possible profit from it. The number of our fellow-creatures killed yearly on our roads is counted in thousands; the number maimed or damaged in tens of thousands. Yet we take pride in the success of the motor industry in creating ever new production records, knowing but ignoring the fact that every increase in the number of cars on the roads involves inevitably a corresponding increase in the destruction of men, women and children. We have come to think that such technological advance must go on; and that any attempt to stop it in the interest of human life is reactionary and inconceivable. We could multiply examples. Some of those from the biological and psychological fields seem to me particularly horrifying. But there is no need. The facts are known to us all, and the interpretation of them which I am suggesting is already clear. The dominance of science, the social priority given to it over other modes of reflection, means the concentration of interest and effort upon technological progress, and so upon the increase of power for its own sake.

From the subjective side this means the dominance of the technological mind. The type of mental outlook which is necessary for the prosecution of scientific research can be adopted as the desirable attitude far beyond the boundaries of science. Where science is dominant this is bound to happen, with greater or less rapidity according to the effectiveness of the opposition that is offered by traditional values and the institutions which embody and maintain them. But the technological advance itself changes social habits and so disrupts tradition. The old forms of valuation become increasingly powerless to control and limit the new forms of power. Moreover, educational procedure will be affected; the schools and universities will be required to transfer the centre of gravity from the arts to the sciences, while the arts themselves are increasingly taught in a 'scientific' fashion. The result is the spread of an attitude to life which sees it as a series of problems to be solved, and for which all problems are techno-logical, and what is needed for their solution is a 'scientific' approach untrammelled by traditional taboos. It is the negative aspect of this that is most important. The concentration of inter-est upon instrumental values involves a growing unawareness of and insensitiveness to intrinsic values; and our sensitiveness to intrinsic values is the measure of our civilization.

What is involved can best be seen if we consider our relations to other people. What would it mean if we were to adopt a scientific or a technological attitude in this field? We should require to be completely objective, unemotional, impersonal. Our knowledge of people would have to be like that of the scientific psychologist, for whom — when he is behaving as a scientist — other people are instances of a type, and their behaviour the exemplification of psychological laws. Intimacy, friendship and personal relationship in the familiar sense are ruled out. Practically, we would treat all people as means to our ends or as obstacles to our purposes. We should seek to discover how to make use of them, or how to defeat and destroy them. We should, in fact, look upon and behave towards other people as if they were things for our use, so far as our power made this possible. The others would, of course, treat us in the same way, and life would be possible in society only through compromise. I leave it to you to fill out the picture for yourselves. There must be few of us who do not know from experience what it is like to be treated in this fashion. I should merely suggest that this spread of the technological mind beyond the proper bounds throws light on many of the social problems of our time. The growth of juvenile delinquency throughout the civilized world, the increase in crime under conditions in which the natural incentives to crime are less than they have ever been, and the imbecilities of the armaments race are obvious instances. But the most complete are the fascist societies. For what we have seen in fascism is a working model of a society in which the extension of the power of the state is the ultimate objective, and any means which is necessary to this end is legitimate and laudable without qualification.

RAS 21–26

– 9 –

The organic analogy

One of Macmurray's main intentions as a philosopher was to challenge and discredit the view that human life can be interpreted in organic terms. The personal includes as its negative element the material and organic but human life cannot be adequately explained by any organic metaphor. Indeed, the application of such a metaphor to social and political theory is positively dangerous, leading towards the totalitarian state.

We must stress first a truth which we have already emphasized from the point of view of the individual. Any human society is a unity of persons. This means that its unity as a society is not merely matter of fact, but matter of intention. It cannot, therefore, be understood, or even properly described in biological terms. It is not a natural phenomenon. It is not an organic unity, even if it has a negative organic aspect.

PR 127

... the thought of the nineteenth century was governed by the idea of organic unity. Life can only be understood in terms of functional relations, and all living complexes are unities of the organic type. For our present purpose the importance of this new concept of the organic individual lies not so much in the field of biology, where it has been supremely successful, but in the field of the human sciences, whether individual or social, in psychology and sociology, and in the philosophy of the State, of morality, and of social life. In this field the substitution of organic for mechanical conceptions completely transformed the situation, and found its classical expression in the organic theory of the State, a theory first sketched out by Rousseau and developed by a line of great philosophers such as Fichte and Hegel in Germany, and Green and Bosanquet in England. In terms of this theory the State is no collection of self-contained individuals held together in a sort of mechanical unity by the operation of

an external force — the power of law; but an organic unity of
individuals, each of whom performs a specific function in and
for the whole, and where variation of function and qualitative
difference in the individuals comprising the State is essential to
the purposive unity of the whole.

A 187f

If the individuals in a society are persons, then from this point
of view the whole which they compose, through their functional
relations to one another, cannot be personal. It must be either
less or more than a person. No organ of the body can be itself
a complete organism. If persons are 'organs' of a social whole,
then the society itself cannot be a person. If the social whole is
a personality, then its individual members cannot be themselves
persons, but only functions of a single personality.

A 189

Behind the Romantic movement there lies a general shift of
interest from matter to Nature. The new idea of Nature is concerned with those features of experience which are peculiar to
the life of organisms, such as growth and reproduction. It is
possible to trace this movement of thought and interest from the
aesthetic field to the philosophical, and from the philosophical
to the scientific; from its first expressions in a highly emotional
and imaginative idealism to the matter-of-fact observation and
realism of evolutionary biology. In this second stage, the crisis
in the effort to overcome social inhibition was the resistance to
the theory of natural evolution. The Darwinian theory which
marks the success of the effort towards a scientific biology was
widely resisted as a challenge to the traditional religious belief
in the creation of the world by God. It is easy to see now that
the resistance was not really religious but drew its strength from
the fear of looking at the facts and so challenging the dignity of
human life. When that resistance had been generally overcome,
and the idea of biological evolution had been accepted, what
had happened was that the strength of customary belief and the
fear of progress had been sufficiently overcome in European
society to enable people generally to look the facts of biology in
the face.

BS 57f

That, however, is the negative side of the cultural movement of Romanticism. On its positive side it turns from man to Nature, and thinks of man as one of the products of Nature, even if he is her highest product. Thus, the 'back-to-Nature' movement is a movement away from man as the centre of significance and interest. Just as the Reformation shifted the focus of culture from God and brought man into the centre of the picture, so the Romantic Revival in turn pushed humanity out of the centre of the picture and brought Nature into focus. The French Revolution, which followed closely upon Rousseau's death, marked in an unmistakable way the success of this movement and the disintegration of humanism.

There is no need for me to labour this point. We are all familiar with naturalism. One has only to take up a volume — any volume — of the poetry which the Romantic Revival produced to see how central the idea of Nature has become, and how human life has faded into its natural background and become an integral part of the greater life of Nature. What we are apt to miss is the relation of this to the whole culture of the nineteenth century and particularly to its social and political developments. Its connexion with democracy we have seen. But it meant equally the development of an interest in history, and particularly in primitive life in all its aspects. Already in Rousseau, we see it leading to the worship of childhood and the apotheosis of the 'noble savage,' for the simple reason that children and primitive peoples are nearer to Nature than civilized adults. This in turn has important practical consequences. The interest in childhood meant the beginnings of the education movements.

The interest in the primitive gave a great impetus to exploration and colonization, and brought about the efforts of the churches and of the industrialists and of governments to bring the backward peoples of the world within the orbit of civilization. On another side, the emphasis on Nature meant inevitably an emphasis upon the natural functions of life. By emphasizing growth it led to the idea of progress, an idea which reduces the significance of human life, whether individual or social, to the contribution which it makes to the future. This brings out clearly how incompatible the idea of progress is with humanism. For the latter is based upon the feeling that human life is significant in itself, absolutely, and not in relation to something beyond itself to which it contributes. But where progress is the central idea in social culture it inevitably reduces the individual to a level of significance where he is merely valuable because of the function he performs in society. That is the price we have had to pay for democracy in order to achieve equality as individuals. We have had to surrender our significance as human beings and become functions in the social organism.

SMMS 26f

Human community

... economic relations, however direct, do not in themselves suffice to establish community between human beings. To these there must be added a mutual recognition of one another as fellows in the sharing of a common life.

I call indirect all relationships which are mediated by something external to themselves, and which are not, therefore, maintained for their own sake. In particular, all forms of relation which are determined by, and which can be defined in terms of, a common purpose, or end to which they are the means, are indirect. Indirect relations are therefore relations of co-operation for the achievement of a common end; and for this reason they admit of organization. They are functional and organic. On the other hand, direct relations are not organic, but personal, and they cannot be organized, since there is no purpose beyond themselves in terms of which they can be determined. They are the direct expression of the inherently mutual or communal nature of man.

All human community is a structure of direct relations between human beings. Community cannot be constituted by indirect relations, or defined in terms of them. It cannot be organic, because it exists, when it does exist, as an end in itself, and there can be no purpose beyond it which can determine it. On the contrary, it generates and determines common purposes. This is immediately evident from the fact that all indirect relations are in principle compatible with a complete absence of community between the persons concerned. I say *in principle* because in practice no set of human relationships that was purely indirect could have any permanence or stability. The positive reason is that, in the absence of a positive impulse to maintain direct relations for their own sake, society would be completely individualist. All motives would be self-regarding, and individuals could only co-operate for the satisfaction of their individual needs.

CSR 523

To say that human life is personal is primarily to deny that human life is organic, or that it can be treated as differing from animal life only in degree and not in kind. It is to assert that the essence of human life is radically different from the essence of organic life, and that the relations which constitute the totality of human life are radically different from those which make a unity of the organic world. It is this essential character of human life, the thing that constitutes its humanness, that Jesus discovered. And what he discovered was already implicit in the Old Testament and had been coming nearer and nearer the threshold of consciousness throughout the process of Jewish development. In trying to understand it we must not forget that it is not merely a reflective generalization. The unity of action and reflection which characterizes religious thinking gives it a fuller meaning than its philosophical form suggests. It means also, 'human life can only be lived personally.'

CH 56

When, therefore, we turn to the problem of our own day, which is, as we have seen, the achievement of an effective world unity, we should bear in mind both principles of human unification. We should remember the relative dissociation of fellowship and co-operation in the process of social development, and the variety of possibilities which their interrelation affords. In particular, we should recognize and oppose, in our own modes of thought and speech, the atavism which infects our modern tradition, and which has been so powerfully reinforced by the influence of biological and evolutionary metaphors. The organic society, with its fusion of co-operation and fellowship on a basis of blood-relationship, lies not at the end, but at the beginning of history. It is what we are moving away from. The patterns of unity in fellowship no longer coincide with or correspond to the political patterns of economic co-operation. Nor is it either possible or necessary that they should.

CF 65

The political unification of Germany, on the other hand, came only very late; imposed forcibly by the military power of Prussia, and necessitated by industrialization. The German State had to be constructed out of a loose confederation of principalities. The basis for this construction was the sentiment of an organic, an almost biological unity of the German Folk. The task was to find a legal and therefore a territorial organization which would embody and express this sentiment of unity.

CF 59

Kinship and nationalism

Under Hitler's leadership, Germany carried nationalism, with its principle of self-determination, to its logical conclusion. By doing so, Germany has proved the bankruptcy of nationalism as a principle of political organization, and has set us the task of overcoming and transcending it. From now onwards nationalism and freedom are incompatible. Their association since the French Revolution, with one another and with the idea of progress, is accidental. In principle, modern nationalism is atavistic; it is a relapse into primitive tribalism; an attempt to reinstate the original organic unity of primitive society as an ideal for civilization. In rejecting nationalism, we are rejecting that worship of the primitive, that glorification of 'nature,' with which the Romantics, from Rousseau onwards, infected modern European culture. We are refusing to be misled, by biological analogies, into substituting an 'organic' society for a human community: and in doing so we are returning to the straight path of civilized development.

It is characteristic of primitive society that the two principles of unity, fellowship and co-operation, define the same group of people. The original kinship-group, from which all subsequent forms of human association are derived, is based upon blood-relationship, upon descent from a common ancestor. Kinship is the basis both of co-operation in work and of fellowship in community. This primitive group is the truly 'organic' society. It is as close to the animal world as human life can come. The artificial element of rational construction is present only in embryo. There is a common life in which all the kin have their part; and reflection is limited to the consciousness of the common life and the expression of this consciousness in the rituals of primitive religion.

CF 61f

The conclusion of the parable [of the Good Samaritan] is that the Jew who fell among thieves, and the Samaritan who helped him, are in community, while the Jew and his own compatriots are not. This conclusion is based upon the fact that the Samaritan shared his material possessions with the Jew in his need, while the priest and the Levite made their natural community as members of the same nation and the same faith an ideal matter which did not express itself in action.

This conclusion cuts very deep into the social question. It rests community between men simply and solely upon a basis of common humanity, and implicitly it negates those so-called natural ties which unite human beings on any basis of special relation. Nationality and organized religion cease to be grounds of human community, and the fact of kindly action overriding those limitations through the simple recognition of the need of another human being is put in their place. This attitude is clinched by what Jesus has to say about blood relationships. 'Who is my mother, and who are my brethren?' he asked; and replied, 'Whosoever shall do the will of my father which is in Heaven, the same is my brother and sister and mother.' Or again, 'I am come to set a man at variance against his father and the daughter against her mother, and the daughter-in-law against her mother-in-law.' In these sayings there is expressed, in an even more striking form, the denial of the natural blood-relationships as the basis of true community. It is in this way that Jesus universalized religion. He conceived human society as based neither on the blood-relationships of natural affinity, nor on the organized relationships of political or ecclesiastical groupings, but simply on the practical sharing of life between any two individuals on a basis of their common humanity. At once there appears the possibility of a unification of all human beings in a single community, irrespective of race, nationality, sex or creed. The Kingdom of Heaven becomes the universal community of mankind based on the sense of unity between man and man, and expressing itself in the sharing of the means of life to meet human needs.

CS 65–67

We are aware today of the totalitarian implications of Rousseau's social theory, particularly in its mature development in
Hegel. Totalitarianism is the result of determining the good as
an object in the spatio-temporal world, and planning its achievement by the use of scientific techniques within a heuristic framework of organic concepts. Kant's condemnation of the attempt
is this, that though it intends a free and self-determining society,
it must necessarily result in destroying freedom, and with
freedom morality and religion, so bringing human personality
under the bondage of a total determination.

Kant could be content to limit knowledge and leave the beyond to faith and hope. For his time a dualism of theory and
practice was possible, and indeed was the path of wisdom. For
us it is impossible. We are committed to planning, whether we
will or not, and planning is the unity of theory and practice
under the primacy of the practical. So long as our most adequate
concept is the organic concept, our social planning can only
issue in a totalitarian society. This is the reason why the emergent problem of contemporary philosophy is the form of the
personal.

SAA 83

Failure of the organic analogy

The root of the error is the attempt to understand the field of
the personal on a biological analogy, and so through organic
categories. The Greek mode of thought was naturally biological, or zoomorphic. The Greek tradition has been strongly
reinforced by the organic philosophies of the nineteenth century and the consequent development of evolutionary biology.
This in turn led to the attempt to create evolutionary sciences
in the human field, particularly in its social aspect. The general
result of these convergent cultural activities — the Romantic movement, the organic philosophies, idealist or realist, and
evolutionary science — was that contemporary thought about
human behaviour, individual and social, became saturated with
biological metaphors, and moulded itself to the requirements
of an organic analogy. It became the common idiom to talk
of ourselves as organisms and of our societies as organic
structures; to refer to the history of society as an evolutionary

process and to account for all human action as an adaptation to environment.

It was assumed, and still is assumed in many quarters, that this way of conceiving human life is scientific and empirical and therefore the truth about us. It is in fact not empirical; it is *a priori* and analogical. Consequently it is not, in the strict sense, even scientific. For this concept, and the categories of understanding which go with it, were not discovered by a patient unbiased examination of the facts of human activity. They were discovered, at best, through an empirical and scientific study of the facts of plant and animal life. They were applied by analogy to the human field on the *a priori* assumption that human life must exhibit the same structure.

The practical consequences are in the end disastrous; but they do reveal the erroneous character of the assumption. To affirm the organic conception in the personal field is implicitly to deny the possibility of action; yet the meaning of the conception lies in its reference to action. We can only act upon the organic conception by transforming it into a determinant of our intention. It becomes an ideal to be achieved. We say, in effect, 'Society is organic; therefore let us make it organic, as it ought to be.' The contradiction here is glaring. If society is organic, then it is meaningless to say that it *ought* to be. For if it ought to be, then it is *not*. The organic conception of the human, as a practical ideal, is what we now call the totalitarian state. It rests on the practical contradiction which corresponds to this theoretical one. 'Man is not free,' it runs, 'therefore he ought not to be free.' If organic theory overlooks human freedom, organic practice must suppress it.

It is one of the major intentions which animate this book to help towards the eradication of this fundamental and dangerous error. It may therefore be advisable, at this point, to issue a flat denial, without qualifications. We are not organisms, but persons. The nexus of relations which unites us in a human society is not organic but personal. Human behaviour cannot be understood, but only caricatured, if it is represented as an adaptation to environment; and there is no such process as social evolution but, instead, a history which reveals a precarious development and possibilities both of progress and of retrogression.

PR 45f

– 10 –

Art as a way of knowing

Macmurray termed science, art and religion 'reflective activities' which deal with different aspects of human experience. Science, in his view, is concerned with 'the world as means' (see Chapter 8) and religion is concerned with the fulfilment of our personal nature through our relations with other people. The function of art is to enable us to appreciate what is of value in itself. For Macmurray it offers a more complete form of knowledge than science does, and engages the emotions. However, he saw art as an essentially individualistic activity and, to that extent, an incomplete form of human expression.

The looking and listening that is characteristic of the artist is more than the seeing and hearing, coupled with a liking or disliking, that we have discussed. The proper name for it is contemplation. The something more than seeing, even than looking, that is involved is an activity of the mind, an attentive considering of what is being perceived. This, however, is still too vague. The considering of the object is not, or is not *merely*, thinking about it. There is no unambiguous language that we can employ to define what is meant: so we must proceed by way of an attempt to describe its essential elements and phases. We shall have in mind, to begin with, the visual arts, reminding ourselves, however, that there is a danger in assuming that all that is true of the arts which derive from an appeal to visual experience will be true of the others — of music, for instance, of dancing or of poetry.

The first element to be noticed is the looking itself. It is systematic, purposeful, critical and usually prolonged. In contemplating an object we are trying to get to know it by means of vision. This should be stressed, because the dominance of science has tended to enclose the very notion of knowledge in a scientific form. We get to know things by looking at them — attentively and carefully. Scientific observation, we notice, passes at once to analysis and generalization. It sees its object from the beginning as an instance of a class; and proceeds to concentrate on its relations to other things. But contemplation, or artistic observation, is quite different. It is concentrated on the object as an individual existent, not as a member of a class. It is said that Japanese landscape artists think it necessary to live for a time in the landscape they intend to paint. They walk about it, watching it at different times of the day, under different conditions of light and in different weathers. This prolonged visual study may last for months, until the painter has thoroughly learned the landscape with his eyes. Then he will shut himself up in his study and paint from memory. Is it really possible to deny that this is a way of *knowing* the world; perhaps, indeed, the only way of knowing anything in its actual individual existence, as distinct from knowing about it? We recognize this most clearly in the case of other human beings, where the distinction between knowing a person and knowing about him is familiar and unambiguous. But the same holds over the whole range of experience. This, then, is the primary element in contemplation. It is our way of getting to know individual things, places, people and so on, by the considered, systematic, purposeful use of our senses.

But sense-perception, however intense and prolonged, is nothing in itself. It is, in abstraction, simply the ideal limit of pure receptivity. In fact, the receptivity of the mind is always the starting-point of activity — the negative element in our doings, as it were. In our practical activity, sense-perception is integrated with our movements as a guide. When we stop to look or to think, sense-perception remains, but as an element in a reflective activity. It is this reflective activity which is the second essential element in contemplation, and it is the character of this element which we have now to consider.

We have an inclination, as a result of our strongly intellectual tradition, to assume that there is only one kind of reflecting, the one which we call thinking or reasoning. In scientific reflection this is, undoubtedly, the kind of activity which takes place. Scientific reflecting is characteristically analytical; it analyses its object into its component parts, refers them to others of the same kind, and draws conclusions for which it offers evidence. It concerns itself little with particular things, but a great deal with relations. It generalizes, and limits itself to matter of fact. We have called this sort of reflection intellectual, for when we talk of the intellect this is the sort of activity we have in mind.

Now the reflective activity in contemplation is not at all like this. It is not an intellectual activity. Scientific reflection results in general theories; and these become the basis of constructive activity through the application of a technical rule which is grounded upon them. But any reflection that results in a theory is not contemplation, and any painting which proceeds by the application of rules is *ipso facto* bad art. Thinking — unless one means by the word simply any kind of 'mental' activity — interferes with contemplation; and the artist must avoid thinking about his work, at least when he is doing it. Instead of being intellectual, the reflective element in contemplation is an emotional activity.

RAS 33–35

Contemplation in art

In what then does the process of emotional reflection consist and how does it express itself? It consists in a critical appraisement of something through a continuous modification of feeling. The appraisement is a search for an appropriate emotional attitude to the object. The process expresses itself in the formation of an adequate image.

To understand this we must get rid of the notion that our feelings are necessarily 'subjective.' You may remember that in talking about the 'objectivity' of thought in science, I suggested that the term 'self-transcendence' might be a better term to use, since the core of objectivity is the capacity to be interested in something for its own sake, and so to set the centre of one's activity outside oneself. The opposite of self-transcendence, then, is egocentricity. Now this self-transcendence is equally characteristic of our feelings, and in particular, of our emotional reflection. Consider the difference between saying of a poem — Milton's *Paradise Lost* for example — that I like it and that it is good. This is quite parallel to the difference between saying that I see the railway lines converging in the distance and saying that the railway lines are parallel. The first statement in each case refers to me and to some modality of my experience. The second refers to the object, quite apart from my experience of it.

The statement of liking or disliking is an expression of immediate emotional reaction to an object. The object acts, as it

were, as a stimulus to my capacity for feeling, and I react positively or negatively. 'I like it' is equivalent to 'it seems good to
me.' But to use this manner of speaking is to recognize that my
liking doesn't settle things. It is problematic. I may be wrong. So
the question arises 'I like it, but is it really good?' Reflection may
alter my judgment or may confirm it. So it is possible that I may
say that 'I like this comedy, but I know that it isn't a good play,'
or 'I know that Milton's *Paradise Lost* is a good poem, but I find
it quite unreadable.' Thus the process of valuation, the passage
from 'I like it' to 'It is good,' is a process in which I get rid of
the reference to my own experience and transcend myself.
Instead of characterizing me, my judgment characterizes the
object. Yet it is my feeling that is the basis of the judgment, so
that the judgment, as in science, remains hypothetical only, and
always liable to revision.

The condition of this process from 'I like it' to 'It is good' is
that I should be interested throughout in the object, and not in
myself being affected by it. My feeling must really be for the
object itself, and the process must be an effort to know and
enjoy the object and not to enjoy myself by means of the object.
This is the essence of emotional self-transcendence, or, if you
will, emotional 'objectivity.' We are, in fact, quite familiar with
the distinction; it is the difference between the way we enjoy a
good 'thriller' and the way we enjoy a great novel. In the first
case what one enjoys is the thrill the story gives us; in the
second it is the book itself, in virtue of its own inherent quality.
Given this concentration of interest in the object the process of
contemplation proceeds by perceptual examination, by discovering more and more of what is there to be perceived, both as to
the elements which make it up and as to the relation of them to
one another in the whole. And as the seeing of it — the knowing of it by critical looking — becomes more adequate, so the
feeling of it — the valuation of it by feeling — becomes corre-
spondingly more adequate. In this process the feeling which is
our first reaction to the object always changes; and it may be
completely reversed. We need only add that throughout the
process our past experience of contemplation plays a decisive
part. The capacity to appraise an object in this way has to be
learned and it grows with exercise.

To describe the process of contemplation is extremely difficult
— perhaps, in the end, impossible. This is because it is not an
intellectual process; it has its own mode of expression which is

by means of imagery, by the construction of images. We might say that it is largely 'unconscious'; that it is not discursive but intuitive; that in the end if our reflection is successful we just know that we are right, but we cannot tell how we know and can certainly not prove that we are right. All this is as it must be and throws no doubt upon the validity of the appraisal, provided, of course, that the conclusion remains hypothetical and subject to continual revision. What the artist can do — and indeed must do — to complete his reflective activity is to create a work of art which embodies it and which submits it to the critical appraisal of other people as well as himself.

The third element in contemplation is then an activity of constructive imagination. In the visual arts it is quite literally the construction of an image; and this image is the painting or the sculpture. It is not, that is to say, a merely mental, but a physical image; and without this externalization of the image the process of reflection is not complete. The process of reflection may, of course, stop short of this: the image may remain private; in which case it remains an unfixed, impermanent and almost certainly unfinished image.

Now this image — which expresses the result of such an emotional reflection — is an appraisal. It is not a reproduction of what, as matter of fact, is seen; certainly not what is seen by everybody. Even in the case of a portrait, the image presented is something quite different from a photograph. It is a judgment upon the sitter, an intuitive valuation which includes, as it must, matter of fact. The portrait must be recognizable, but the art of the cartoonist reveals how little is necessary by way of statement for this purpose. The rest is characterization. To express this appraisal the artist must isolate the object from its relations to other things, eliminate what, in ordinary perception, is merely general, and therefore adventitious to the individuality of the object, and express the object in the image as an integral whole, existing in its own right. This is what I meant by talking of the construction of an adequate image. Just as science generalizes, so art individualizes its object, and through this individualizing presents it as a self-existing entity, complete in itself.

The technique by which this adequacy of the image is achieved is one of selection, modification and organization. The image, if it is to present the object in its individuality, must itself be self-contained. This is what is meant by saying that a work of art is an organic whole. The elements of which it is composed are not merely arranged; they are organized. They are functionally or purposively related to one another, so that they give the impression of necessity. What this secures is that the composition of the image is such that the elements refer us to one another, and so are seen as constituting a completed whole, which needs nothing beyond itself for its apprehension. Its formal characters, therefore, are rhythm, proportion, balance and harmony.

I have confined myself in this commentary upon art to the visual arts. The whole range of art includes very great differences, and any complete picture would require to consider each of them in turn. This is clearly impossible in the time at our disposal, and to a great extent beyond the range of our immediate purpose. If any of you feel that you want to say, 'This may be all very well for painting, but how about music and dancing, poetry and drama, architecture and the rest?,' I can only reply that I am aware of these and have taken them into account; and I believe that what I have selected for comment in the case of the visual arts has its proper counterpart in all the others, and that the account I have given will apply, *mutatis mutandis*, to any. The most difficult application is to music, which has a non-representational character that sets it apart. About this I would make one comment. The difficulty is parallel to that presented by pure mathematics in the case of the sciences. Music seems to have the same relation to the other arts that mathematics has to the other sciences, and there is some evidence to suggest that mathematics is itself derivative from music.

But there is a final consideration that should be included in our discussion, and which may help to answer this natural doubt. I have talked throughout about the 'object' of contemplation. It would be a mistake to interpret this to refer only to 'things' that are seen. By an 'object' in this connection I mean much what John Locke meant by an idea — whatever is before a man's mind when he thinks. It must, of course, be something which can be exhibited or symbolized in sensuous terms. But is there anything at all that is excluded by this proviso? It does not exclude patterns of sound or colour or movement. It does not even exclude general ideas so far as these are apprehended in their sensuous or imaginable embodiments or symbols. It can make room for the wildest fantasies of the dream world. What matters is only that there should be something which sets going the process of contemplation, which gives rise to a reflection which is not intellectual but emotional and which moves to an expression which isolates and individualizes, instead of generalizing and relating.

Before indicating the practical function of the arts, a word is necessary about the contemplative attitude which is required for all artistic activity. The essential point, in which the contrast with the scientific attitude is very clear, is that the subject is individualized equally and reciprocally with the object. The artist, that is to say, cannot work to a rule without ceasing to be an artist. He sees the object in its individual uniqueness, and is himself individualized in the process. He must express the object *as he sees it*, and the uniqueness of his seeing is necessary to the success of the artistic process. The scientist, we saw, seeks to minimize the personal factor. He wants to see as everybody sees. The artist maximizes the personal element. Music is the most impersonal of the arts. Yet it is in music that it is easiest to recognize the composer from hearing the music he has written. This refusal to see the world through the eyes of others, this being true in the smallest detail to his own vision and his own feeling, is what the artist means by being honest. The use of general rules of technique instead of the immediacy of personal apprehension is a trickery which vitiates the effect. The expressions, therefore, which different artists find for the same object are themselves different; and the difference of interpretation is a hallmark of artistic genuineness. It is not a defect, and it does not mean, as we are too ready to suppose, that art is subjective. Properly understood it is a guarantee of artistic objectivity.

We have already noticed that the contemplative attitude is intuitional and emotional, in contrast with the intellectuality and discursiveness of science. We need add only that the activity of the artist does not exclude the intellectual processes in the way and to the extent that science excludes the emotional activities. Art subordinates the intellectual processes of analysis and inference and generalizing relatively to those of contemplation. The subject matter of a poem can be scientific. But it is in the preparation for the essential phase of contemplation, in determining the techniques of expression and so forth that thinking is useful. A famous teacher of art, commenting on the drawing of the human figure, advised his pupils to study anatomy thoroughly and then forget it. This embodies the proper relation between science and art in the practice of art. We should perhaps add that there is an aesthetic moment in scientific discovery — a flash of insight that fuses a mass of data and reveals the law of their unity — which is indispensable. But it is subordinated immediately and strictly to the scientific demand for generality and experiment.

The relation of the arts and their production to the common life of everyday action is, as one would expect, totally different from that of science. Science, we saw, extends our capacity for action by providing the basis of technologies; so determining the rules of technical procedure. Art is concerned, however, with the exhibition of values, and, therefore, in relation to action, with the choice of ends. It cannot, however, affect action by the provision of rules; if only because the choice of ends is a matter of intuition and feeling, not of discursive thought. If art is to function in the development and improvement of primary activity, it must be by its effects upon our capacity for sensuous and emotional discrimination. The practical function of art is, therefore, the refinement of sensibility. Any product of art implies 'This is good' as any statement implies, 'This is true.' So art involves always a discrimination between good and bad: and the more penetrating the reflection which it expresses, the more valid this implication is. So it sets standards and moulds the unconscious to an immediacy of acceptance and rejection. It is an education of emotion and a training of judgment.

RAS 37–42

Because Macmurray did not regard the emotions as inherently irrational, he believed that they can, in principle, be educated. Artistic appreciation, and the disciplined expression of creativity, were for him important ways of enabling such education to occur.

How, then, are we to educate and develop our emotional life so that we can trust our feelings to reveal the values of the world to us? To answer that question I must begin by drawing attention to an aspect of our experience which is too much overlooked and yet in which the root of the whole matter lies. I refer to the use we make of our senses and of our sense-experience. The education of our emotional life is primarily an education of our sensibility.

RE 37

The fundamental element in the development of the emotional life is the training of this capacity to live in the senses, to become more and more delicately and completely aware of the world around us, because it is a good half of the meaning of life to be so. It is a training in sensitiveness; which is a very different thing from accurate observation. The reason is that awareness is directly related to action and that our modes of awareness determine our modes of action. If we limit awareness so that it merely feeds the intellect with the material for thought, our actions will be intellectually determined. They will be mechanical, planned, thought-out. Our sensitiveness is being limited to a part of ourselves — the brain in particular — and, therefore, we will act only with part of ourselves, at least so far as our actions are consciously and rationally determined. If, on the other hand, we live in awareness, seeking the full development of our sensibility to the world, we shall soak ourselves in the life of the world around us; with the result that we shall act with the whole of ourselves. The author of a recent book [*A Life of One's Own,* by Joanna Field], in explaining how she discovered this in her own experience, says that she found herself listening to music through the soles of her feet. If you have any inkling of what that means you will understand me when I say that we have to learn to live with the whole of our bodies, not only with our heads. If we do this, we shall find ourselves able to act in the world with the whole of our bodies, and our actions will be spontaneous, emotional, non-mechanical and free. Intellectually controlled action, in fact, is only possible through the process of inhibition. The intellect itself cannot be a source of action. All motives of action are necessarily emotional, but the intellect can use the emotion of fear to paralyse the positive emotions, leaving only that one free to determine action which corresponds to the planned purpose. Such action can never be creative, because creativeness is a characteristic which belongs to personality in its wholeness, acting as a whole, and not to any of its parts acting separately.

RE 44f

Discipline really involves not subordination but integration. It aims at co-ordinating all the elements in personality and creating a harmonious unity in which they all co-operate freely and without hindrance. Any human action involves the co-ordination of innumerable activities. The capacity to walk or even to stand upright involves a co-operation of muscle and nerves which has to be established gradually through training and experience. If this is true of these simple activities, how much more is it of the higher types of skill which constitute the peculiar capacities of human beings, and which in their totality we call reason. The human body and mind together contain the potentiality of the development of behaviour which is the expression of skill in action almost infinitely diverse in its variety and incredibly intricate in its mechanism. Such skilled behaviour can only be realized through discipline, through the integration of a multitude of simple capacities which are trained to act together harmoniously to a single end. To secure this integration is the essence of real discipline. Its achievement is shown in the freedom and grace of action; in its rhythmic quality; in the absence of jerkiness and effort. These are the external signs of discipline. The inner signs are the feelings of freedom and joy and ease in action which testify that all the necessary factors are co-operating harmoniously in the production of the desired effect. But we must remember that human activity is essentially a co-operation between individuals and that the discipline which will produce a human result must succeed not merely in integrating the various capacities of the individual but in integrating individuals themselves in a community of free co-operation.

RE 83f

– 11 –

The errors of individualism

We have seen earlier (see Chapter 2) that Macmurray rejected the Car-
tesian idea of the isolated, thinking Self. The human person is
embodied, and expresses himself or herself through physical action. In
Macmurray's view there can be no such thing as an isolated Self.
Human experience is irreducibly reciprocal, and any isolated Self is an
abstraction from the inter-personal world in which we all grow up and
form a sense of identity.

... [The child's] existence and its development depend from the
beginning on rational activities, upon thought and action. The
baby cannot yet think or act. Consequently he must depend for
his life upon the thought and action of others. The conclusion is
not that the infant is still an animal which will become rational
through some curious organic process of development. It is that
he cannot, even theoretically, live an isolated existence; that he
is not an independent individual. He lives a common life as one
term in a personal relation. Only in the process of development
does he learn to achieve a relative independence, and that only
by appropriating the techniques of a rational social tradition. All
the infant's activities in maintaining his existence are shared and
co-operative. He cannot even feed; he has to be fed. The sucking
reflex is his sole contribution to his own nutrition, the rest is the
mother's.

PR 50

There must, however, be a positive side to this. The baby must
be fitted by nature at birth to the conditions into which he is
born; for otherwise he could not survive. He is, in fact, 'adapted,' to speak paradoxically, to being unadapted, 'adapted' to a
complete dependence upon an adult human being. He is made
to be cared for. He is born into a love-relationship which is
inherently personal. Not merely his personal development, but
his very survival depends upon the maintaining of this relation;

he depends for his existence, that is to say, upon intelligent understanding, upon rational foresight. He cannot think for himself, yet he cannot do without thinking; so someone else must think for him. He cannot foresee his own needs and provide for them; so he must be provided for by another's foresight. He cannot do himself what is necessary to his own survival and development. It must be done for him by another who can, or he will die.

PR 48

The infant and mother

Now so far as concerns behaviour which is adapted to a natural environment, the human infant does not behave at all. Its movements are conspicuously random. If this were all, we should have no grounds for suspecting the presence of motives, or indeed of consciousness. The baby's movements could quite well be described as automatisms. What prevents this conclusion is an observable progress, with no conspicuous breaks, in the direction of controlled activity. The movements gradually lose their random character and acquire direction and form. But the character of this development is quite unlike that observable even in the highest animals. It does not rapidly produce a capacity to adapt itself to the environment. In the early stages, at least, it does not seem to tend in this direction at all. It is quite a long time before the baby learns to walk or to stand or even to crawl; and his early locomotion, so far from making him more capable of looking after himself, increases the dangers of his existence, and the need for constant parental care and watchfulness. Nature leaves the provision for his physiological needs and his well-being to the mother for many years, until indeed he has learned to form his own intentions, and acquired the skill to execute them and the knowledge and foresight which will enable him to act responsibly as a member of a personal community.

PR 52f

It has commonly been asserted that what distinguishes us from the animals is the gift of speech. There is an obvious truth in this, but it has two defects if used for purposes of definition. The

power of speech is sometimes defined as the capacity to express
ourselves. This misses an essential point; for the power of
speech is as much the capacity to understand what is said to us
as it is to say things to other people. The ability to speak is then,
in the proper sense, the capacity to enter into reciprocal communication with others. It is our ability to share our experience
with one another and so to constitute and participate in a common experience. Secondly, speech is a particular skill; and like
all skills it presupposes an end to which it is a means. No one
considers that deaf-mutes lack the characteristic which distinguishes them as human beings from the animals. They are
merely obliged to discover other means of communication than
speech. Long before the child learns to speak he is able to communicate, meaningfully and intentionally, with his mother. In
learning language, he is acquiring a more effective and more
elaborate means of doing something which he already can do in
a crude and more primitive fashion. If this were not so, not
merely the child's acquiring of speech, but the very existence of
language would be an inexplicable mystery. Nor should we
forget that he learns to speak by being spoken to; he is taught
to speak, and he understands what is said to him before he is
able to respond in articulate words.

It would, of course, be possible to find, in animal life, instances in plenty which seem to be, and perhaps actually are, cases
of communication. To take these as objections to what has been
urged here would be to miss the point. For these are not
definitive. In the human infant — and this is the heart of the
matter — the impulse to communication is his sole adaptation
to the world into which he is born. Implicit and unconscious it
may be, yet it is sufficient to constitute the mother–child relation
as the basic form of human existence, as a personal mutuality,
as a 'You and I' with a common life. For this reason the infant
is born a person and not an animal. All his subsequent experience, all the habits he forms and the skills he acquires fall within
this framework, and are fitted to it. Thus human experience is,
in principle, shared experience; human life, even in its most
individual elements, is a common life; and human behaviour
carries always, in its inherent structure, a reference to the personal Other. All this may be summed up by saying that the unit
of personal existence is not the individual, but two persons in
personal relation; and that we are persons not by individual
right, but in virtue of our relation to one another. The personal

is constituted by personal relatedness. The unit of the personal is not the 'I,' but the 'You and I.'

We can now define the original motivation-pattern of personal behaviour. We have recognized, as the minimum of our original motive consciousness, the capacity to feel comfort and discomfort. But the behaviour which is motived by this distinction is, we now see, an activity which communicates the experience to the mother. The motivation of the infant's behaviour is still bipolar; it has a positive and a negative phase; the negative phase being genetically prior, since it expresses a need for the mother's aid, while the positive expresses satisfaction in the supply of its needs. But both the negative and positive poles have an original and implicit reference to the other person, with whom the infant shares a common life. This original reference to the other is of a definitive importance. It is the germ of rationality. For the character that distinguishes rational from non-rational experience, in all the expressions of reason, is its reference to the Other-than-myself. What we call 'objectivity' is one expression of this — the conscious reference of an idea to an object. But it is to be noted that this is not the primary expression of reason. What is primary, even in respect of reflective thought — is the reference to the other *person*. A true judgment is one which is made by one individual — as every judgment must be — but is valid for all others. Objective thought presupposes this by the assumption that there is a common object about which a communication may be made.

The human infant, then, being born into, and adapted to, a common life with the mother, is a person from birth. His survival depends upon reason, that is to say, upon action and not upon reaction to stimulus. We must, therefore, complete our analysis by defining it in its positive personal mode, which contains and is constituted by its negative or organic aspect. The animal has certain needs — for food, for warmth, for protection. It is endowed by nature with specific patterns of behaviour for their satisfaction. The child has the same needs; but it is not so provided. Instead, it has a single need which contains them all — the need for a mother, the need to be cared for. If this need is satisfied the organic needs are provided for. The baby does not feed himself, he is fed. He does not protect himself, he is protected. The provision for his various needs falls within the mother's care as aspects and manifestations of it. They differentiate her caring and give it actuality and systematic form. The baby need do nothing about his organic needs, and therefore need not even be aware of them discriminatingly. Now the positive motive of the mother's caring is her love for the child; it contains, however, and subordinates a negative component of fear — anxiety for the child's welfare. This negative component is essential, since it provides the motive for thought and foresight on the child's behalf, and for provision in advance against the dangers to its life, health and welfare, both in the present and the future. Without it love would be inoperative and ineffectual, a mere sentimentality and therefore unreal.

Now since the mother–child relation is the original unit of personal existence, the motivation of the child's behaviour must be reciprocal, even if this reciprocity is, to begin with, merely implicit. The positive and negative poles of the infant's motivation are the germinal forms of love and fear respectively. The sense of discomfort expressed in the call for the mother is implicitly the fear of isolation; and since isolation from the relationship which constitutes his existence, if it lasts too long, means death, it is implicitly the fear of death. The sense of comfort communicated by his expression of delight in being cared for is the germinal form of love. This bipolar, reciprocal, love and fear motivation is concerned with maintaining the personal relationship in a common life between mother and child. We need draw attention only to two characteristics which have a special importance for our further study. The first is that the negative pole, in the child's behaviour as in the mother's, falls within and is subordinated to the positive. Isolation from the mother, if it becomes permanent, does involve death. The baby who loses the mother loses his life. But the fear of isolation functions in the child's life as a means of bringing the mother's care into active operation and so eliminating the ground for fear. It diversifies the child's experience of the relationship, and institutes the rhythm of withdrawal and return to which I referred in the first volume [*The Self as Agent*, p.181]. The second characteristic is this. There is from the beginning an element of symbolic activity involved which has no organic or utilitarian purpose, and which makes the relationship, as it were, an end in itself. The relationship is enjoyed, both by mother and child, for its own sake. The mother not only does what is needful for the child: she fondles him, caresses him, rocks him in her arms, and croons to him; and the baby responds with expressions of delight in his mother's care which have no biological significance. These gestures symbolize a mutual delight in the relation which unites them in a common life: they are expressions of affection through which each communicates to the other their delight in the relationship, and they represent, for its own sake, a consciousness of communicating. It is not long before the baby's cries convey, not some organic distress, but simply the need for the mother's presence to banish the sense of loneliness, and to reassure him of her care for him. As soon as she appears, as soon as the baby is in touch with her again, the crying ceases, and is replaced by a smile of welcome.

PR 60–63

Now the original unity which is developed in this way is a relation of persons. It is the unity of a common life. The 'You and I' relation, we must recall, constitutes the personal, and both the 'You' and the 'I' are constituted, as individual persons, by the mutuality of their relation. Consequently, the development of the individual person is the development of his relation to the Other. Personal individuality is not an original given fact. It is achieved through the progressive differentiation of the original unity of the 'You and I.' If this sounds difficult or paradoxical, it is yet a commonplace in some of its manifestations. We all distinguish ourselves, as individuals, from the society of which we are members and to which we belong. The paradox is the same: for we at once assert ourselves as constituent members of the society while opposing it to ourselves as the 'other-than-I.' So the child discovers himself as an individual by contrasting himself, and indeed by wilfully opposing himself to the family *to which he belongs;* and this *discovery* of his individuality is at the same time the *realization* of his individuality. We are part of that from which we distinguish ourselves and to which, as agents, we oppose ourselves. In this — which is, indeed, simply another manifestation of the form of the personal — we may find the answer to many of the questions which puzzle the moralist; the existence of conscience, for example, of responsibility and the moral struggle; or, more generally, of the capacity which is possessed by a person, and only by a person, to represent his fellows — to feel and think and act, not for himself but for the other.

PR 91

Macmurray rejected any individualistic conception of religion. Since religion is about personal relationships and the quality of communal life, any philosophy or social outlook which is individualistic is to that extent a denial of religious faith and practice.

We must refer also, with similar brevity, to individual, in contrast to corporate, religion. This aspect is an essential one, though it is secondary. 'Religion,' said Whitehead, 'is what a man does with his solitariness.' This dictum expresses a modern tendency to emphasize the individual aspect at the expense of the corporate; a tendency which flows from and strengthens the individualism of much of our Western outlook. But individualism, like the idealism which tends to accompany and complete it, is finally incompatible with religion, if only because it is incompatible with the inherent relatedness of personal life. The individual phase of personal relation, the necessary withdrawal into the self and so into solitariness, refers to the return to community and is for the sake of that return. Its religious aspect must always have relation to corporate religion if it is to function religiously. In formal terms, a relation to God which is not a relation to my neighbour is unreal. The withdrawal of the individual into religious solitude, into prayer and meditation, into self-examination and self-dedication, is an affirmation of his personal dependence, not an escape from it.

RAS 69f

Tribes unite into cities, cities into nations, nations into empires; and throughout history the range of effective human community increases — in depth as well as breadth. That is the religious development of mankind. Wherever you find the effort to achieve human equality, to overcome the enmities and self-interests that separate individuals and classes and nations and races, you are discovering the working of religion — of religious reason — in man. You find it, for example, at the basis of modern communism, for all its profession of atheism. You find Karl Marx describing the whole stretch of human history from the breakdown of primitive tribal communism to the establishment of universal communism — the unification of all nations and races in the community of the world — which is his apocalypse, the brotherhood of men that is to be — you find him describing the intermediate stage, as the result of the estrangement *(Entfremdung)* of Man from himself, from his own reality;

and the establishment of communism as the reconciliation of man with himself. That is religious insight — partial and incomplete, but essentially religious. For the great negation of religion is individualism, egocentricity become a philosophy; and it is inherently atheist, however much it says 'Lord, Lord!'

RE 64f

The world of the individualist is one of fear, and leads to defensiveness, isolation and self-frustration.

The discovery that all objectives have the same illusory character is the experience of *despair*. It is expressed in the judgment that human life is inherently meaningless and that all action is futile.

A categorial misconception is a misconception of one's own nature. Error in theory involves failure in practice. This is the principle on which all verification rests. If, however, the error lies in our conception of our own nature, it must affect all our action, for we shall misconceive our own reality by appearing to ourselves to be what we are not, or not to be what we are. The result can only be a self-frustration based upon a self-deception. Under these conditions, Kant's conclusion is correct. We know ourselves only as we appear to ourselves and not as we really are. This expresses itself in action as self-frustration. Our actions appear to be determined, though they really are free. But this is only true in virtue of a negative motivation in relation to other persons. For then action is defensive and appears to be dictated by the other person, against whom I must defend myself. In reality it is determined not by him but by my fear of him. Thus, when two friends quarrel and are estranged, each blames the other for the bad relations between them. Or, to put it otherwise, if my motivation is negative then I appear to myself as an isolated individual who must act for himself and achieve whatever he can achieve by his individual efforts, in a world which cares nothing for his success or failure. Yet in reality, my isolation is a self-isolation, a withdrawal from relationships through fear of the other. This attitude, which expresses the experience of frustration and despair, is nothing but the sophisticated adult version of the attitude of the child whose mother refuses to give him what he wants. Its unsophisticated formula is, 'Nobody loves me.'

PR 149

– 12 –

The value of emotion

*We have already seen that Macmurray did not accept the common
identification of reason with intellect (see Chapter 4). In his view, both
intellect and emotion can be either rational or irrational. Despite his
own intellectual gifts, Macmurray considered the emotions more important than the intellect in determining the quality of personal life. It
is therefore important to educate the emotions, since they provide a
means of knowledge and perception.*

... if reason is the capacity to *act* in terms of the nature of the
object, it is emotion which stands directly behind activity
determining its substance and direction, while thought is related
to action indirectly and through emotion, determining only its
form, and that only partially.

RE 26

What we feel and how we feel is far more important than what
we think and how we think. Feeling is the stuff of which our
consciousness is made, the atmosphere in which all our thinking
and all our conduct is bathed. All the motives which govern and
drive our lives are emotional. Love and hate, anger and fear,
curiosity and joy are the springs of all that is most noble and
most detestable in the history of men and nations. Scientific
thought may give us power over the forces of nature, but it is
feeling that determines whether we shall use that power for the
increase of human happiness or for forging weapons of destruction to tear human happiness in pieces. Thought may construct
the machinery of civilization, but it is feeling that drives the
machine; and the more powerful the machine is, the more
dangerous it is if the feelings which drive it are at fault. Feeling
is more important than thought.

FMW 146

The emotional life is not simply a part or an aspect of human life. It is not, as we so often think, subordinate, or subsidiary to the mind. It is the core and essence of human life. The intellect arises out of it, is rooted in it, draws its nourishment and sustenance from it, and is the subordinate partner in the human economy. This is because the intellect is essentially instrumental. Thinking is not living. At its worst it is a substitute for living; at its best a means of living better. As we have seen, the emotional life is our life, both as awareness of the world and as action in the world, so far as it is lived for its own sake. Its value lies in itself, not in anything beyond it which it is a means of achieving.

RE 75

Now, of course, it is difficult to be sincere — much more difficult than we usually imagine. But the point I wish to draw your attention to is this: that though we are sensitive to the moral need for intellectual insincerity, we are very insensitive to the need for emotional sincerity. We may excuse mental insincerity under certain circumstances, but we never, I think, would praise it as a virtue. Yet we constantly inculcate emotional insincerity as a duty, and praise people for concealing their real feelings, or pretending to feelings that they do not possess. We pretend to like the things that we are told we ought to like; we pretend that we feel sympathy for a person in distress, when we do not, and we not only see no harm in this, but we positively encourage it as a social virtue. In reality emotional sincerity is far more important than the sincerity of the mind, because it lies nearer to the heart of life and conduct. It is vicious to pretend about our feelings. It is something of which we ought to feel ashamed.

One other point we must notice. We know that a man who habitually trifles with the truth tends to lose the capacity to distinguish between truth and falsehood. It is dangerously easy to deceive ourselves about what we believe. If we keep repeating a story that is not true we come to believe in its truth ourselves. Now this holds good with even greater force in the emotional life. If we habitually cheat others about our feelings, we soon become unable to know what we really feel. If we act as though we love a person when we do not, we will come to believe that we do love him. If there is any truth about life that experience and modern psychology have together driven home to me it is this — that any pretence about our feelings results in self-deception. We become incapable of knowing what we really feel. I have heard Christian moralists say that the way to learn to love people whom you dislike is to behave to them as if you loved them. This, I am certain, is completely and dangerously false. Emotional pretence leads to emotional insensibility. If you express systematically to anyone, in word or action, a love which you do not feel, you will undoubtedly come to believe that you love him. But you will hate him without knowing it. That is what the psycho-analyst discovers. To tamper with the sincerity of your emotional life is to destroy your inner integrity, to become unreal for yourself and others, to lose the capacity of knowing what you feel.

RE 130f

Uncontrolled feelings, like loose thinking, can lead us into error. But even strong emotions, such as love or hatred or anger, may sharpen the focus of our attention, quicken our apprehension of the object upon which they are directed, and lead to the recognition of truths, and even of facts, which otherwise would have escaped our notice.

PR 33

Intellect and emotion

The tradition of our civilization is heavily biased in favour of the intellect against the emotions. We think that it is wise to trust our minds, and foolish to trust our feelings. We consider that it is the human intellect that raises man above the level of the animal creation, while the emotional movements in us are what gives us kinship with the animals. We behave in terms of that bias. Faced with a problem, we invariably turn to the intellect to solve it for us. If we find that what we have done has landed us in difficulties, we immediately assume that we must have miscalculated, that we didn't think the thing over with sufficient care. In many cases, and these the most important, the mistake lies not in our thinking but in our feeling. It is not our thinking that was false, but our emotion. As a result we admire and rely upon all those expressions of human life which are intellectual — science, law, power, duty, machinery and so on, and we spend much time and labour on the task of developing our intellects and training our capacity to think; while we hardly ever think it necessary, or even possible, to train our capacity for feeling.

This bias in favour of the intellect has a long history behind it. Its roots lie in that very ancient doctrine that teaches the evil of desire and the necessity for subduing desire. It is only another expression of the same doctrine that looks upon the body as itself evil, as the prison-house of the pure spirit which is corrupted and infected by its contact with matter. We have softened down the crudeness of the expression of this view in modern times, but it is still true, I think, that it governs us to a much greater degree than we imagine. It still determines our emotional attitudes, even while we repudiate it in our thoughts. We still *feel* that there is something ignoble about the body, just because it is the body, and that a bodily desire is disreputable somehow, just because it is bodily. The citadel of this ancient organization of feeling against the body is, of course, our attitude to sex. In that field our lives are dominated by feelings which are quite irrational, which refuse to combine with our intellectual convictions and with the spirit which we approve in other fields. The result is that we are nearly all obsessed by sex, and unable to solve the practical dilemma that it sets us throughout a large part of our lives.

FMW 44f

... we have set the intellect free and kept emotion in chains. That is a summary of the inner history of the modern world. The driving force below the development of Europe has always been the struggle for freedom, and the clue to that struggle lies in Christianity. Freedom, of course, means responsibility. To live freely is to be responsible for one's own life; and everything in us that seeks to shirk that responsibility fights against freedom. During the Middle Ages the desire to escape responsibility was too strong for the growing desire for freedom, and so both the intellectual and the emotional life remained in bondage to external authority. The ends of life and the means of achieving these ends were both imposed upon men; what was to be desired and what was to be thought were both determined for men; and the demand for freedom of life, which Christianity had implanted and which was growing in secret and seeking to be born, was drugged by promises of satisfaction in another world, and so diverted from the effort to realize freedom in this world.

FMW 48

There is a point at which the freedom of thought is incompatible with the bondage of the emotional life. And we have reached it. Up to a point it is possible to keep our thought and our feeling separate. Up to a point it is possible to keep truth and value separate. But there comes a point at which the freedom of thought turns back upon ourselves and begins to ask, 'What are the facts about your own feelings? Are your feelings about what is good and beautiful and useful compatible with the facts of the world as we now know them?' That is the point at which history has placed us. We can only maintain our dogmatic certainty of conviction by setting limits to the freedom of thought to enquire honestly into the standing of our convictions. We must either set our emotions free or destroy the freedom of thought.

That is my conclusion. We are standing, to-day, at the second crisis of our European history; the second great crisis in the fight for human freedom. The first was the crisis in which we chose, after much fear and hesitation and persecution, to trust one another to think for ourselves and to stand by the expression of our honest thought. Now we are called upon to implement that faith in the human mind by trusting in the integrity of human feeling. I shall go on to deal with the religious significance of this new demand upon our faith. But I should like to say one other thing first. To trust our human feelings and act upon them freely is not to do as we feel inclined. It is not to feel anyhow and to act anyhow. The free thought that has unravelled the mysteries of the natural world is not and cannot be undisciplined thought, which is never free. Scientific thought is thought set free to discover what is true and to believe the truth that it discovers, however much it may upset existing opinions. It is disciplined by the world with which it deals, by testing its conclusions against fact. The freedom of our emotional life is to be achieved only on the same conditions: that we set out to discover, through feeling, the real values of our world and of our life in the world. We shall have to submit to the discipline of our feelings, not by authority nor by tradition, but by life itself. It will not guarantee us security or pleasure or happiness or comfort; but it will give us what is more worth having, a slow, gradual realization of the goodness of the world and of living in it.

FMW 52f

Macmurray believed that the Roman influence in European thought had led to a denigration of the emotions, and that the flourishing of the arts during the Renaissance could be interpreted as a revolt against that influence. A second revolt occurred three centuries later with the upsurge of Romanticism.

The second great eruption of the Greek and Christian elements in our tradition, the second revolt against the dominion of law and intellect, occurred towards the end of the eighteenth century. We call it the Romantic Revival. Though it was notably an artistic and literary phenomenon, it had profound effects in every department of European life and thought and worked a vast revolution in our tradition. In politics it produced Rousseau and the modern democratic State. In social life it produced the educational and humanitarian movements. In philosophy it produced Hegel and modern idealism. In science it produced Darwin and evolutionary biology. In religion it produced the higher criticism and undermined the authority of the Bible. In economics it produced Karl Marx and socialism. This complete transformation of life had its roots in an outburst of emotional spontaneity. Its high priests were the Romantic poets with their pure emotional lyricism.

We must try to estimate the effect of Romanticism upon the dominant Stoic tradition of Europe. Did it succeed in dethroning the tradition of Roman will and in releasing the emotional life from its subservience to rational principles? It did not. The Roman dominance re-established itself, but precariously and only through compromise. It granted the demands of emotion in theory and then proceeded to make its concessions ineffective in practice. And in doing this it introduced a pretence into the life of Europe which has poisoned it to this day. Our emotional life was set free in word, but not in fact. This is the origin of sentimentality. The second revolt of the Greek–Christian elements against the dominance of the Roman sentimentalized the moral and social life of Europe.

Sentimentality

We must content ourselves here with a few examples which will illustrate this. Sentimentality is emotion which is unreal, though it thinks it is real; which is unfree though it thinks it is free.

Now we are familiar with this in a thousand forms. Indeed it is still the very texture of our social life. In politics we pretend that we govern ourselves, that democracy is 'government of the people, by the people, for the people.' In fact, of course, it is nothing of the sort, and in the nature of things it could never be. Yet the power of government to do its job of making and administering the law depends upon its capacity to make people feel that it is merely doing what they want it to do. The elaborate machinery of political campaigns is designed to arouse and maintain an emotional state of public opinion which will 'authorize' the politicians to do what they have already decided to do on quite different (and usually much sounder and saner) grounds.

We are worked up into a state of feeling in which we are easily persuaded that what we want done is what the politicians think ought to be done, so that the acts passed by Parliament subsequently can be said to express the will of the people. This is sentimentality in politics, for which the politicians are not really to blame. For it is we who demand that the pretence shall be kept up. The effect of it is that we imagine that we are free to determine the political conditions under which we live when in fact they are determined for us by rational necessity.

The simplest and most straightforward example of this sentimentalizing of emotion is the romantic treatment of love. The Romantic movement produced something like a deification of love, as we all know; and this the moral tradition of Europe accepted. But it accepted it on the tacit condition that it should remain the servant of social order and continue to work for the rational ends of organization, stability and efficiency. In religion the pretence was that love of God meant serving humanity. But if that is so, why bother about God or religion? In the social field, love of one's fellows was made to mean the service of humanitarian causes and self-sacrifice in the interest of a common good. But if what you want is to secure the triumph of a cause or the improvement of social conditions, why bother about loving people? All you have to do is to organize them and drill them into social efficiency. So in the sphere of sex-love, though there was an elaborate pretence that the true basis of relationship between men and women was spontaneous affection, the nineteenth century took even more elaborate pains to prevent this emotional ideal from governing conduct. The machinery of hypocrisy presided over by Mrs Grundy was a very effective device for sentimentalizing emotion, for keeping it ineffective in practice, for directing it into the service of the ideals of social life prescribed by a rational tradition.

FMW 87–90

– 13 –

Fear

By fear, Macmurray was not referring to our instinctive response to danger, but to a mistrustful attitude towards the world, which may be expressed in habitually defensive or aggressive reactions. For Macmurray, one of religion's chief functions is to enable us to overcome fear, and it was his conviction that the life and teachings of Jesus show how this can be achieved.

The primary fear of death of its very nature must generate a pervasive attitude of defence against everything and everyone. It is life itself that is the source of death, and a consciousness pervaded by the fear of death is continuously on the defensive against life and isolated from life. There are from the beginning two main forms of this isolation, though they are closely bound up together. The consciousness of death isolates man from Nature, since Nature is one of the main sources of danger. It also isolates man from his fellows, turning them into potential enemies who may destroy his life. Salvation from the fear of death must thus include the reintegration of the individual with his fellows and the reintegration of man with Nature, in the light of the full consciousness of death. This is the task of religion. In animal life, the community of the individual with all life and with Nature is unbroken because it is instinctive. With the appearance of man that continuity is broken and the individual is forced into isolation; standing over against a world of men and Nature against which he must defend himself, and against which he knows he cannot defend himself.

CS 39

The root problem of human action lies here. Fear is unlike all the other emotions because it is negative. It is not a positive motive for action, but a motive for the inhibition of action. The permanent pervasion of consciousness by fear signifies the continuous presence of an impulse to refrain from action and to suppress it. There is thus a close psychological connexion between fear and death in human behaviour. Life is activity, and depends upon the continuous presence of positive motives for action. Death is the natural suppression of the activity in which life consists. Fear is the presence in a living consciousness of the suppression of the life-activity.

CS 46

The immediate and necessary effect of the conquest of fear by reason is that the people in whom it is achieved find themselves trusting and loving one another. The creation of human society depends on this. The process of social development depends upon maintaining, extending and deepening the range and quality of this trust and love, through the continuous conquest of fear.

CS 100

These considerations bring us to the heart of the question. What is the solution which Jesus discovered for the problem of fear? There can be no doubt that he was throughout concerned with it. There are numerous expressions which show that he looked upon fear and the isolation and self-defence to which it gives rise, as unnatural. He expresses amazement at the lack of faith which he finds among men. It leads him into expressions of an almost exaggerated intensity. 'If ye have faith,' he says, 'as a grain of mustard seed ye shall say to this mountain, "Be thou removed and be thou cast into the depths of the sea," and it shall be done.' Faith is his name for that attitude of consciousness which is completely triumphant over fear, for which the world is home and there is no sense of isolation or helplessness. Faith is for him the natural condition of human consciousness and it expresses itself in the control of the material world.

CS 109

... this brings us back to his diagnosis of the human problem as the predominance of fear over 'faith' or trust and so to the question how fear in man is to be overcome.

The answer to fear is love. The reason is expressed in the First Epistle of John, 'There is no fear in love, but perfect love casteth out fear.' Love and fear are indeed the two primary personal motives, the one positive and the other negative. Life is a going out to the 'other' and this going out in interest and care is its positive content. Fear paralyses the flow and turns us back upon ourselves. The other becomes a danger against which we must defend ourselves. Such self-defence is the negation of personal life. This is the meaning and purpose of Jesus' 'new commandment' to his disciples to 'Love one another.'

Does this take us any further? If fear is not cured by telling people not to be afraid; is love produced by telling people to love one another? No, it is not; yet the situation is not so hopeless in this case. Love is the fulfilment of life, and so is natural. Fear, the same Epistle tells us, has torment; and love offers an escape from the torment of fear. This is enough to make us wish to escape from fear, but not to deliver us. But there is a farther power in love that can. Love tends to call out its own response. If we are loved, we tend naturally to return the love, through the natural reciprocity which belongs to personal life in its positive manifestations. So Jesus adds something to the announcement of his new commandment. 'Love one another,' he says, 'as I have loved you.' And the answer is also in the record: 'We love him because he first loved us.' Indeed, to make it more sure, he links his command to the personal infinite, saying 'As the father hath loved me, so have I loved you. Continue ye in my love.'

This then is Jesus' answer to the problem of fear as a dominating human motive, which makes faith impossible.

PJ 11

From fear stems hatred, resulting in the deliberate negation of personal relationships, and in consequent self-frustration.

The first point that claims our attention is the derivation of a third original motive from the interrelation of the positive and negative motives in the personal situation. As we have identified the first two by reference to the emotions of love and fear, we can identify the third by reference to hatred, but with the same caution. In some respects it might be better to use the term 'resentment' instead of 'hatred'; though in that case we should have to replace 'fear' by 'anxiety,' and 'love' by 'caring' — since the term 'charity,' which would be the corresponding word, has been debased in usage. I call this motive original because, like love and fear, it is a universal component in the relation of persons, inherent in the personal situation in all its forms. I call it derivative because it presupposes love and fear as operative motives. It originates in the frustration of love by fear, through the mutuality of the personal relation. The behaviour which expresses love requires, for its completion, a response from the other to whom it is directed. Love is fulfilled only when it is reciprocated. If the response is refused, the action which expresses the positive motive is frustrated. Now, in general, the personal relation is unavoidable, since the personal is constituted by the personal relation; and the refusal of mutuality is the frustration of personal existence absolutely. This can be seen in the original mother–child relation in its stark simplicity. If the mother refuses to care for the child, the child must die. But when a rejected lover commits suicide the motivation is the same. The act is irrational because there are other alternatives open for the fulfilment of his personal life. In general, however, and in principle, the 'You and I' relation which makes us persons is such that if you act positively to me, so offering to enter into friendly relations, and I reject your advance, I threaten your existence as a person in an absolute fashion. I throw you back on yourself, and the negative pole of your motivation must become dominant. You are afraid for your own personal existence, which is threatened by my motivation in relation with you. Consequently you necessarily resent my action; and if the relation is unavoidable then your resentment becomes hatred — a persistent motive in your personal relation to me; not, of course, we must remember, a persistent *emotion* which you feel towards me. Hatred, therefore, as an original motive is inevitable in all personal relations, though, like the other motives, only as a component of a complex motivation, not necessarily dominant, and subject to the control of intention. It is inevitable, because it is impossible that you should always be able to respond to me in the way that my action expects. This is why forbearance and forgiveness are necessities of positive personal relationship. The rejection of personal relationship itself is a negative aspect of personal relationship, and itself enforces a reciprocity of negation. In so far as I threaten your personal fulfilment you can only reciprocate by threatening mine. Hatred, therefore, is the emotion by which we can identify the motive of mutual negation in the personal relation. If it completely escapes from intentional control it issues in murder. For this reason we contrast love and hatred as opposites rather than love and fear. Both have a direct reference to the Other. They sustain a positive and a negative relation of persons respectively. Yet the opposi-

tion of love and fear as contraries is more fundamental. For a
negative relation of persons is a practical contradiction. It is a
relation which is at once maintained and refused, and which is
therefore inherently self-stultifying. It can only be maintained by
a positive motive: its rejection can only mean that this positive
motive is continuously inhibited by a negative one. Now we
have seen that a positive relation of persons must contain and
subordinate a negative element: the possibility of a negative relation can only signify an inversion of this motivation in which
the negative element is dominant and subordinates the positive.
Hatred therefore, is a motive of self-frustration. Since the 'You
and I' relation constitutes both the 'You' and the 'I' persons, the
relation to the 'You' is necessary for my personal existence. If,
through fear of the 'You' I reject this relation, I frustrate my own
being. It follows that hatred cannot, as a motive of action, be
universalized. It presupposes both love and fear, and if it could
be total it would destroy the possibility of personal existence. It
is no doubt this that underlies, even if it does not completely
justify, our tendency to assume that suicide is evidence of mental derangement.

                                                      PR 73–75

Fear against life

It is worth while noting that it is only rarely in individuals and
more rarely in societies that human life exhibits itself in its
proper nature, when it is not mastered and inhibited by fear.
Average human life is not normal. For the viciousness of fear is
that it sets our life against itself. When we concentrate on defending ourselves against the world outside us, against nature
and other nations and other people, we are frustrating ourselves;
and the more successful we are in achieving security, the more
completely do we frustrate ourselves. For what are we afraid of?
What are we defending ourselves against? Against life — against
our own life, the life that is us. There is only one secure defence
against life, and that is death. The person who lives on the
defensive is really seeking death, seeking to escape from life.
And most of us succeed only too well, and wake up late in life
to discover that we have never really lived at all.

The effort to defend oneself against life is inevitably self-defeating in the long run. For the defences we build round our precious selves only serve to isolate us from all that we really want. There is no fear more potent than the fear of fear, which is the fear of isolation. The more we defend ourselves against life the more we feel isolated from life and the more deadly becomes our fear. We are in a vicious circle; for this fear of isolation only drives us to strengthen our defence-mechanism, and so to isolate us still more. Now, there is one kind of defence to which I must draw your attention, because of its importance and its peculiar deadliness. It is the provision of what the psychologists call escape-mechanisms, but which is more simply called pretence or make-believe. We resort to imaginary activities and pretend they are real ones. For example, we pretend that we are enjoying life by working ourselves into a state of excitement. We slap one another on the back and call one another by our Christian names to pretend that we are really in touch with one another, and to cheat the feeling of emptiness and isolation that gnaws at our vitals. And the sociability, the energy and activity that we create in this way is spurious. It commits us to unreality. It is the expression of our fear of being alone, not of our love of being together. It is the activity of death, not of life, and to anyone who has eyes to see it gives itself away by its mechanical nature. Every real expression of life is an expression of positive spontaneity and works from within outwards. If we are really alive we are love-determined and live outwards into the world. But every real expression of life has its counterfeit, its imitation, which is based on fear; and fear is the disease, the one root-disease of human life.

FMW 60f

Now when people grow afraid, when there is a secret hidden fear at the centre of their consciousness, they have lost faith in themselves, and they begin to clutch at anything to save them. And they turn always to power, especially to organized power. They want an authority to take the burden of responsibility off their shoulders. They become formalists in religion and morality. They get excited about money and position because they want to be safe and secure. They want everybody to agree with them, because then they feel safe in their beliefs. That is when the false morality of obedience to law becomes rampant. People want an authority to tell them what to do, to make them feel safe.

FMW 213

– 14 –

Politics and law

Much political debate this century has concerned the role of the State. Macmurray believed that, at its worst, the State attempts to impose unity by force, but that at its best it is a means of ensuring justice in society.

We are apt to think that politics is the exercise of power, and that the State works through compulsion and constraint. The fact which gives colour to this opinion is that alone among institutions the State has the right to use force to secure obedience to its commands. This fact, however, is easily misunderstood. The purpose of the State is the elimination of the use of force in human intercourse. We arrange, therefore, that if force *must* be used, it shall be used *only* by the State. Nor do we stop there. We go on to secure that it shall be difficult for the State to use force; that it shall be used, even by the State, only after due process of law, and only as a last resort when all else fails. The intention of politics is not the use of force, but the elimination of force and the achievement of freedom through justice.

CF 33

... there are many instances of self-supporting and self-sufficient human societies which cannot, or can only with difficulty, be subsumed under the concept of the State. We might instance primitive tribes, the Hebrews of Old Testament times, China before its modernization by revolution, and so on. The idea of the State is closely linked with the idea of power, and the symbolism of the State is predominantly military. We talk indeed of States as Powers — whether great Powers or smaller Powers. It seems doubtful whether what we call the city-states of ancient Greece were really States in our sense of the term. For us the State is a legal entity, whose limits are defined by the territorial boundaries of its legal authority. Yet even an idealist philosopher like Bosanquet, who is concerned to deny that society is based on force, and to maintain that its unity is a spiritual and not a material unity, entitles the work in which this thesis is so brilliantly sustained, *The Philosophical Theory of the State.*

This modern tendency to identify society with the State, or at least to define society through the aspect of political organization, is strong evidence of a dominantly pragmatic apperception of the social bond. For we recognized the mode of morality which rests upon a pragmatic apperception by the central place it gives to the ideas of 'power' and 'law.' The historical explanation of this identification is not far to seek. We are the heirs of the Roman tradition; and the Romans, whose outlook was characteristically pragmatic, invented the State as we know it. They did this by conceiving law as a technology for keeping the peace, and by uniting in one society, by the administration of a homogeneous law backed by force, peoples and tribes who were in most other respects, and especially in culture, heterogeneous. As a result, we tend to think that organization as a State is the criterion of a fully complete and mature society, and to treat societies which lack this character either as dependent groups within a State, or as immature and undeveloped societies which must, like minors, be educated into statehood under the tutelage of their adult neighbours.

PR 133

Power as end in itself

Law then is a technological device, and the State is a set of technical devices for the development and maintenance of law. Now the value of any device lies wholly in its efficiency. To personalize the State, to assign it the religious function of creating community, to make it an end in itself and ascribe to it an intrinsic value, is, in fact, to value efficiency for its own sake. It is to make power the supreme good, and personal life a struggle for power. This is the height of unreason. For power is merely a general term for the means of action. To make power an end is to invert the logical relation between means and end. This is indeed possible, and in certain circumstances justifiable. For there are types of power which are general, in the sense that they can be used as a means to a number of different ends. Consequently, it is possible to intend the accumulation of power without deciding in advance what end it shall be used to secure. The accumulation of wealth, the accumulation of knowledge, the accumulation of territory and many other general means of action can be pursued for their own sake, simply by postponing the question of the use to be made of them in the long run. But if the question is not postponed but ignored, there arises a conception of power as an absolute end, and corresponding to it a way of life which consists in the exploitation of power for its own sake. The right thing to do becomes whatever the available means makes possible.

The State is a device, we have said; but we must now add that it is a necessary device which cannot be dispensed with or exchanged for any other, so soon at least as the necessary co-operation in society requires an adjustment of indirect human relations. Both Aristotle and Rousseau recognized that the condition of the free society which was their ideal depends upon all its members being able to meet together in one assembly and so to be in direct relation with one another. A mere extension of numbers to the point where this becomes physically impossible makes law enforced by the State the only means of escaping anarchy; the only way in which the peace can be kept. This necessity for politics gives the State a special character as a device. It is a device which is necessary beyond an early stage of social development for the very possibility of civilized human existence. This invests the State with an absolute character which other devices do not possess, and which gives it a claim upon us which they cannot have. Without justice, social co-operation is impossible, without law, justice is impossible and without power law is futile and ineffective, a mere ideal. We have therefore a moral obligation to maintain the law and to secure its efficiency.

But the necessity of law, even its absolute necessity, makes no difference to its pragmatic character; it tends rather to make the misuse of law more dangerous. For if the apperception of any society becomes predominantly pragmatic; if power becomes the end rather than the means, then the power of the State becomes absolute, since it is the power which determines, through law, the exercise of all power. The will to power necessarily results in the apotheosis of the State: for it makes the State the author of society and society the creature of the State. Law becomes not the means to justice but the criterion of justice. Morality becomes the system of actions which maintain and increase the power of the State; and this the State alone can determine. Moreover, the indirect or economic relations of persons then become their defining characters; every man is a centre of power at the command of the State, and the use to which he is put is for the State to decide. If the State has no use for him then he has no value, and therefore no right to live. This is the genesis of great Leviathan, 'that mortal God,' as Hobbes calls it, to which we owe our being and our defence. But we do not need to turn back to Hobbes to recognize the beast, accurate though Hobbes's description of him is. We ourselves, in our generation, have assisted at his rebirth.

Leviathan is not merely a monster, but a fabulous monster; the creature of a terrified imagination. If we track the State to its lair, what shall we find? Merely a collection of overworked and worried gentlemen, not at all unlike ourselves, doing their best to keep the machinery of government working as well as may be, and hard put to it to keep up appearances. They are, like ourselves, subject to the illusion of power. If we expect them to work miracles, we flatter them, and tempt them to think they are supermen. If we insist that it is their business to make peace on earth and hand us the millennium on a platter, what will happen? Those of them who are wise enough to know their limitations, and to be immune to the gross adulation of their fellows, will resign; and government will be carried on only by megalomaniacs, who are capable of believing themselves possessed of superhuman attributes and whose lust for power is the measure of their weakness. There is no need to wonder how it comes about that a neurotic visionary like Hitler can come to control the destinies of a great nation, nor that he uses his power in a mad fury of meaningless destruction. We know quite well that this is how fear works in human relations. We have discussed already, in considering the relation of mother and child, that interplay of love and fear that generates hatred, and finds its natural expression in destructive fury. What we forget is that the State is merely a set of devices to make law and to make it effective, and that law is a device for securing justice. Like any device it can be misused. It can be used to perpetuate or to extend injustice. The problematic of politics works in terms of the antithesis of 'just' and 'unjust.' The problem is to see that the devices of government are used only for the purpose for which they are designed.

PR 198–201

During the Second World War Macmurray gave two lectures in which he attempted to define a form of democracy to replace the nineteenth-century identification of it with laissez-faire economic doctrine. He argued that socialist policies are not inevitably totalitarian: as long as religious and cultural freedom are guaranteed the State cannot command the citizen's complete allegiance. Such freedom is not in any case guaranteed under capitalism, since cultural life will tend to be influenced by economic forces which are not subject to any social or political control.

Democracy, as we understand the term in this country, is the denial of the omnicompetence of government. The opposite of democracy is, therefore, Totalitarianism, which rests on the claim of the State to have rightful authority in every department of human life. The principle of the natural limitation of the authority of the State raises the questions which underlie the development of democratic freedom and of democratic institutions: What are the proper limits of political authority, and, how can the State be effectively confined within these limits in the exercise of its power? The second reason why the recognition of the freedom of religion from political control is fundamental is that it implies more than appears at first sight. It implies, in principle, the freedom of all cultural activities from State control. It implies freedom of conscience, freedom of thought, freedom of learning and of art and literature — in a word, all that is involved in freedom of mind. The implications of religious toleration run through all our democratic liberties — freedom of speech, freedom of thought, freedom of the press, of cultural association, of public criticism, and propaganda. For it accepts the principle that the man is more than a citizen, and that the State is merely an aspect, and not the most important aspect, of the community.

CD 11f

The spiritual life — the culture of the individual or of the community — can be distinguished from the material life, but in actual fact they cannot be separated. Without material resources we cannot live. Without adequate material resources, the personal life must remain stunted and undeveloped. The economic activities of a community are the indispensable basis for its cultural life The means of life are also the means of a good life. The purpose of democracy in limiting the authority of government is to set free the personal and cultural life of the community and its members; and the necessity for this lies in the fact that freedom is the life blood of all culture and the condition of the good life. Now, if the economic life of the community is excluded from the control and direction of a democratic government, then there is no way by which the community can secure for all its members the means of realizing the cultural freedom which it is the purpose of democracy to make possible. The means of *exercising* the freedoms that democracy assures to its members are distributed by the chances of economic success or failure in free competition. This means, in effect, that the realization of the good life depends upon relative wealth. Whoever controls wealth controls the means of cultural development and personal freedom.

We noticed that the development of industrialization tends to concentrate material resources under the control of a decreasing number of people. It follows that in the highly industrialized stages of a negative democracy the control of culture which democracy denies to political authority is exercised in fact by economic powers which are themselves exempt from political control. The freedom of the economic life becomes incompatible with the freedom of the cultural life. Economic freedom negates cultural freedom: the spiritual life comes into bondage to the material life, and the purpose of democracy is frustrated. When such a stage is reached the free economy of negative democracy has become incompatible with democracy and tends to destroy it.

CD 21f

Since human life is personal, and the personal includes the organic and the material, human activities are justified only in so far as they enhance the quality of personal relationships. When personal considerations are outweighed by economic factors the means have become ends in themselves — an irrational state of affairs. Similarly, the law must not become an end in itself, since it is only a means of achieving justice; and justice is a bare minimum of moral behaviour without which a fully personal morality is impossible.

... we must turn our attention to this negative aspect of the general theme, and consider persons in indirect relation. Broadly speaking, this negative aspect is economic. But it is the negative aspect of a society of persons, and is, therefore, intentional. It is an intentional co-operation in work, that is, action directed upon the world-as-means, to the corporate production and distribution of the means of personal life in society. This co-operation in work establishes a nexus of indirect relations between all the members of the co-operating group, irrespective of their personal relations, whether these are positive or negative or non-existent. Such relations are not relations of persons as persons, but only as workers; they are relations of the functions which each person performs in the co-operative association; and if this aspect of the personal is abstracted, and considered in isolation, every person is identified with his function. He *is* a miner, or a tinsmith, or a doctor, or a teacher.

Now this economic aspect of the personal — the working life — is both intentional and for the sake of the personal life. As intentional, it is not mere matter of fact. It must be produced, maintained and developed by deliberate effort. As negative — being for the sake of the personal life to which it is the means — it requires to be justified by reference to the personal life which makes it possible. In itself, the economic nexus of relation is purely pragmatic. Its standard is efficiency, and its problematic is in terms of efficiency and inefficiency. Its aim is to deliver the goods, in the maximum quantity, quality and variety for a given expenditure of labour. From the economic point of view, every person is a potential source of energy and skill to be used with the maximum of efficiency in the mechanism of production. He is himself a means to an end, and this end is the production of the means of life. It is, therefore, not self-justifying; it must be judged as a whole by the place it plays in the personal lives of all the workers. An economic efficiency which is achieved at the expense of the personal life is self-condemned, and in the end self-frustrating. The mobility of labour, for example, is a good thing from the economic point of view. It is a condition of efficiency in the system of production. From the personal point of view, it is an evil, though it may be justified under special circumstances as the lesser of two evils. For the mobility of labour means a continuous breaking of the nexus of direct relations between persons and between a person and his natural environment; and it is on the continuity of these relations that the development of the personal life must depend. The more mobile the workers are, the more frequently they are cut off from their roots, and forced to grow new ones. The end result can only be the destruction of the family and the production of the 'mass-man.' At the same time the economic field is, for all workers, a field of necessity, not of freedom. The work must go on, irrespective of the particular intentions and motives of the workers. Every worker must perform his allotted task, whether he wants to or not, either freely, because he likes doing it, or under constraint, because he is afraid of the consequences if he does not. Economic activity is in principle a routine of action which has to be maintained; which has to be adapted to the resources available, both material and technical; which has to be made as efficient as possible; and finally, which has to be subordinated and adjusted to the personal life of society as a whole, and to the personal lives of all its members. Necessity is for the sake of freedom: the economic is for the sake of the personal. This maintaining, improving and adjusting the indirect or economic relations of persons is the sphere of politics. Its institutional expression is the state, and its central function is the maintaining of justice.

Now justice is a moral idea. Yet when we consider its place in the system of moral ideas it exhibits a curious ambiguity. From one point of view justice is so meagre and universal a virtue that it seems hardly to be a virtue at all. It expresses the minimum of reciprocity and interest in the other in the personal relation — what can rightly be exacted from him if it is refused. We contrast it with mercy, with generosity, with benevolence, with all these moral qualities which express a positive readiness to sacrifice self-interest for the sake of others. I can demand justice for myself from others, and even enforce it, but not bene-volence or generosity or affection. In such conditions justice seems essentially negative; a kind of zero or lower limit of moral behaviour. On the other hand, justice can appear as the very essence of morality without which the higher virtues lose their moral quality. To spend the money that should have paid my debts unselfishly upon those whose need touches my sympathy is positively immoral; and the mother who devotes her care and affection to one of her children at the expense of the others is a bad mother. The care for another which fails in justice loses its moral character, whatever other moral qualities it may display. From this point of view, justice seems to be the *sine qua non* of all morality, the very essence of righteousness, in a sense the whole of morality.

If we take both these aspects together, we have another ex-ample of the form of the personal. Justice is that negative aspect of morality which is necessary to the constitution of the positive, though subordinate within it. Morality can only be defined through its positive aspect, yet it can only be realized through its own negative. Without justice, morality becomes illusory and sentimental, the mere appearance of morality. The reason for this lies quite clearly in the fact that justice safeguards the inclusiveness of the moral reference, and so the unity of the Other. To be generous without being just is to be generous to some at the expense of others; and so to produce a minor mutuality which is hostile to the interests of the larger community. It is to create and defend a corporate self-interest, and this destroys the universality of the moral reference. To be more than just to some and less than just to the others is to be unjust to all.

PR 186–89

Achieving justice

But is such a concept as 'absolute justice' ever meaningful, any more than a concept of absolute mercy would be? If all parties to a bargain are satisfied with their bargain then the arrangement is fair to them all. Justice, after all, is the negative aspect of morality only, the minimum of morality which can be demanded as necessary to the co-operation of free agents; the negative of habitual rightness in action without which all the positive aspects of morality lose their rightness.

Law may be misused, as we have seen. But it may also be inadequate as an instrument for its purpose. One aspect of this inadequacy is of special significance at the present time. The presupposition of law is an economic nexus of indirect relations which constitutes a *de facto* unity of co-operation. For this reason law will be inadequate to its purpose unless all the persons whose actions affect one another, and so may give rise to injustice, come within the scope of a single system of law. Where trade develops between independent States to a point at which their citizens become interdependent in a settled system of economic relations, there is created a society without a common law to secure justice between its members. The various independent systems of law are then incapable of securing full justice even within the territories which determine their limits. Each separate State must seek to use its power to control the whole economy of which it is only a part in the interests of its own citizens. So law is perverted into an instrument for the defence of privilege, and for the perpetuation of injustice. Unless the independent States can unite, by common consent, under one system of effective law, they must destroy one another in a struggle for power. This happened in ancient Greece; and destroyed the Greek way of life. It is happening today on a scale that involves the whole world.

The principle which governs such a situation is this. Without justice, co-operation becomes impossible. If the co-operation is compulsory it must then become a co-operation in mutual self-destruction. This is merely a restatement on a large scale of the principles of personal motivation which we discovered in the relation of mother and child. The dominance of negative motivation in the relation of persons destroys the possibility of friendship and finds its ultimate and natural expression in an effort to destroy the other. In the political field the condition of avoiding this catastrophe depends upon intending justice: and this is incompatible with the worship of the State, which is the worship of power. The symbol of this worship is the personification of the State, and for this reason it is all important that we should treat the law, and the State which is the creature of law, for no less but also for no more than it is — a necessary system of devices for achieving and maintaining justice. If we do this, we will then realize that justice itself is not enough. For justice is only the negative aspect of morality, and itself is for the sake of friendship.

PR 204f

– 15 –

Morality

Macmurray, as we have seen, did not accept mechanistic and organic interpretations of human behaviour (see Chapter 3). Morality cannot therefore, in his view, be based on obedience to laws or to the greater good of some evolutionary process.

... morality cannot consist in obedience. To obey is to try to throw the responsibility for our actions on someone else; and that is to deny our own humanity.

But equally, the idea of morality is inconsistent with the idea of law. The root idea of law is consistency and uniformity. Everybody must do the same thing in the same circumstances. If our activities were governed by law they would be invariable, always the same; and such activities would of course be mechanical. If there were such a thing as a moral law then a perfectly good man would be an automaton, a mere robot, with no human freedom at all. The more mechanical life becomes, the more it is organized by law, the less human it is. To be moral means to be as completely human as we can be; and our human nature is, as we have seen, our capacity to think really and feel really for ourselves, and to act accordingly. The more our actions are governed by laws, the less freely we can act, the less room there is for us to think and feel really and so be ourselves. The more law there is in our lives, the less morality there is. That is why I insist that the morality of obedience and law is a false morality, a mechanical morality.

How does it come about, then, that so many people talk about morality as if it consisted in obeying a moral law? I will give you two answers: the first a very plain practical one; the second a deeper and more theoretical one.

If everybody else acted in obedience to a fixed law, then they would act with uniform consistency. We should then know what everybody would do in all circumstances. We could tell beforehand what to expect of them and we should never be let down.

We could lay our own plans with complete safety and know that nobody would upset them by doing something unexpected. And that would be so much simpler and more satisfactory for us. So we want everybody to be consistent. We want them to recognize all sorts of fixed duties, to pledge themselves to do things in a way that will bind them for the future. We even go so far as to require people to promise that they will love and honour us all their lives. Why? So that we can be secure, and certain of the future, and lay our own plans for the future with safety. The real reason for wanting people to be consistent is just that we may be able to count on them, to calculate their behaviour beforehand. That is why we tell people that there is a moral law and they ought to obey it. It is really for our own supposed advantage. And you will notice that this making of laws to govern people's conduct is really an attempt to turn people into machines, to make them behave like material bodies, like the sun and the stars. And to do that is to attempt to destroy their freedom, to deny their human nature; and — to put it in another way — it is to refuse to trust them. If you trust people you don't try to bind them.

That brings me to the more general answer. People who talk of obeying the laws of morality are treating human beings as if they ought to behave like material objects. Material bodies are free, as we have seen, in obeying laws. That is because it is the nature of matter to obey laws. Now we are all so familiar with science and scientific ways of thinking that we have a tendency to think of everything in scientific terms. So we say to ourselves, 'There must be a law governing human behaviour just as there is a law governing the courses of the stars.' We then look at the facts of human life and find that it isn't so; that some people are rebels, and that nearly everybody has lapses at times. So we say, 'Well! if human nature doesn't always behave in accordance with fixed principles, that is just because it is wicked. It *ought* to follow a strict law of good behaviour.' So we come to think that there is a law of good behaviour which we ought to obey even if we don't always obey it. And we think that the better and more moral a man is, the more he does in fact obey the moral law.

What is wrong with all this? Simply that it makes the mistake of thinking that human nature is the same as material nature. It isn't. Material nature is free in obeying laws. Human nature is bound or enslaved in obeying laws. It is not the nature of human beings to act in conformity to law, and therefore their goodness — which we call morality — cannot consist in obedience to law at all. That is not to say that there is no place for law in human life. It means simply that there is no place for law and obedience in morality. Human life has a material basis and a material aspect, and *there* is the place for law. But in the true personal life of human beings, in which alone they express their full nature as moral beings, there is no place for mechanism or obedience.

FMW 189–92

Now suppose that we apply these biological ideas to human life so as to produce a conception of how we ought to behave. We shall then produce a kind of biological morality. How will it talk about human goodness? Let us see. It will talk a great deal about purpose. Each of us ought to have a purpose in life and to work for its achievement, it will say. Then whatever draws us aside from our purpose will be bad and whatever advances it will be good. Stage by stage we must use our opportunities and develop our capacities with our eyes fixed on the goal to which we have devoted our lives. We must admire the single-mindedness of the young man who sets out to become a millionaire, and who sacrifices pleasure and comfort, toiling year after year for the accomplishment of his purpose, adapting himself to circumstances, devoting himself to success. But after all, that is a selfish purpose, even if we admire the self-sacrifice and single-mindedness of the man. There is something ridiculous about a man toiling all his life for a success which he never will have time to enjoy. Why is that? Because he is forgetting that he is a member of a community, that he is a mere individual whose life is a momentary part of the great stream of life. His purpose is too limited. If human life is to be good, it must not forget that the purpose which it serves is not its own purpose but the purpose of life as a whole.

So this second false morality has to look beyond the individual to the community, just as the biologist has to look to the species and the development of the species. We must begin over again from the larger standpoint. Each of us is born into a society and our lives are bound up with the community to which we belong. Human goodness is a common goodness, a social goodness. Life has been transmitted to us by our parents and all our capacities are inherited capacities. Society gives us nourishment and education and the opportunities of self-development. We owe all we have and all we are to the community to which we belong. The community is our real environment, and we live only in it and through it. Therefore the purpose which ought to control our lives is not our own selfish purpose, but the social purpose. We are part of a community of social life, and the goodness of our individual lives depends upon our devoting them to the common good. Each of us has a place and a function in society. Our business is to take our place in the social organization and devote ourselves to our task. So the ideal of social service arises, and social morality. The good man is the man who serves his country, serves his generation, identifies himself with the good of the community and devotes his life to the accomplishment of a social purpose.

FMW 195f

On sexual matters Macmurray took the view that since morality is about the quality of personal relationships, sexual ethics are a matter of emotional sincerity rather than of obedience to moral laws.

The morality of the relations between men and women has nothing to do with the differences of sex, which belong to the physical and the organic, not to the personal plane. The proper relations between human beings are personal relations, in which organic differences have no essential standing. Difference of sex is on the same level as differences of natural capacity. Therefore, men and women must meet and enter into relationships on the personal level — not as male and female, but as human beings, equally made in the image of God. They must determine their relations to one another for themselves, as human persons, and not allow organic differences to determine their relations for them. There is only one proper ground of relationship between any two human beings, and that is mutual friendship. Difference of sex may make the friendship easier or more difficult of achievement, but it cannot make any difference in principle.

Further, if difference of sex is made an essential difference in human relations, then men and women are treated as complementary to one another. Each, then, has meaning and significance only in terms of the other. Neither is a real individual. Now this is a denial of human personality. It destroys the possibility of true friendship between them. Complete individual integrity is the condition of personal relationship. Otherwise you inevitably subordinate persons to their function. Moral relations are dependent on the absolute value of the human being, as a free human spirit, not as a man or a woman.

RE 134f

Now take another point. There is only one safeguard against self-deception in the face of desire, and that is emotional sincerity, or chastity. No intellectual principle, no general rule of judgment is of any use. How can a man or woman know whether they love another person or merely want them? Only by the integrity of his or her emotional life. If they have habitually been insincere in the expression of their feelings, they will be unable to tell. They will think they love when they only want another person for themselves. What is usually known as 'being in love' is simply being in this condition. It blinds us to the reality of other people; leads us to pretend about their virtues, beauties, capacities, and so forth; deprives us of the power of honest feeling and wraps us in a fog of unreality. That is no condition for any human being to be in. If you love a person you love him or her in their stark reality, and refuse to shut your eyes to their defects and errors. For to do that is to shut your eyes to their needs.

Chastity, or emotional sincerity, is an emotional grasp of reality. 'Falling in love' and 'being in love' are inventions of romantic sentimentality, the inevitable result of the deceit and pretence and suppression from which we suffer. Love cannot abide deceit, or pretence or unreality. It rests only in the reality of the loved one, demands the integrity of its object, demands that the loved one should be himself, so that it may love him for himself.

This indicates the true basis for *any* intimate personal relationship and applies universally between persons, whether they are of the same or of different sexes. What then of the morality of sexual intercourse? It falls, in the first place, within the wider morality of personal relationship of which we have been speaking, and is governed by it. Any intimate human relationship must be based upon love and governed by that emotional sincerity which is the essence of chastity. Real personal love is the basis in the absence of which specifically sexual relations are unchaste and immoral. This holds inside marriage just as much as outside it. The fact of marriage cannot make chaste what is in itself unchaste. I would hazard the guess, without much fear that I was wrong, that there is as much sexual immorality inside marriage as outside it. Morality does not rest on externals.

In the second place, between two human beings who love one another, the sexual relationship is one of the possible expressions of love, as it is one of the possible co-operations in love — more intimate, more fundamental, more fraught with consequences inner and outer, but essentially one of the expressions of love, not fundamentally different in principle from any others, as regards its use. It is neither something high and holy, something to venerate and be proud of, nor is it something low and contemptible, to be ashamed of. It is a simple ordinary organic function to be used like all the others, for the expression of personality in the service of love. This is very important. If you make it a thing apart, to be kept separate from the ordinary functions of life, to be mentioned only in whispers; if you exalt it romantically or debase it with feelings of contempt (and if you do the one you will find that you are doing the other at the same time; just as to set women on a pedestal is to assert their inferiority and so insult their humanity); if you single out sex in that way as something very special and wonderful and terrible, you merely exasperate it and make it uncontrollable. That is what our society has done. It has produced in us a chronic condition of quite unnatural exasperation. There is a vast organization in our civilization for the stimulation of sex — clothes, pictures, plays, books, advertisements and so on. They keep up in us a state of sexual hypersensitiveness, as a result of which we greatly overestimate the strength and violence of natural sexuality. And the most powerful stimulant of sex is the effort to suppress it. There is only one cure, to take it up, simply, frankly and naturally into the circle of our activities; and only chastity, the ordinary sincerity of the emotional life, can enable us to do so.

Sex, then, must fall within the life of personality, and be an expression of love. For unlike all our other organic functions it is essentially mutual. If it is to be chaste, therefore, it must fall within a real unity of two persons — within essential friendship. And it must be a necessary part of that unity. The ideal of chastity is a very high and difficult one, demanding an emotional unity between a man and a woman which transcends egoism and selfish desire. In such a unity sex ceases to be an appetite — a want to be satisfied — and becomes a means of communion, simple and natural. Mutual self-satisfaction is incompatible with chastity, which demands the expression of a personal unity already secured. Indeed, it seems to me, that it is only when such a unity in friendship has reached a point where it is shut up to that expression of itself that it is completely chaste.

RE 137–40

Personal relationships are possible regardless of social and racial differences, Macmurray believed, through the simple fact of shared person-hood. Morality is therefore a matter of recognizing that person-hood and treating all humans as equal.

The primary difference in the relation of persons to persons which distinguishes it *toto caelo* from the other types of relationship is its mutuality. In this case that to which I relate myself is of my own order. The other is my equal, my fellow. If I meet him, he meets me, in the same personal sense. We meet as man to man. This is the basic fact about the objective situation in which one human being relates himself to another. It is no theory, no mystical ideal, but the simplest fact of human experience. And it suffices to define the nature of rationality in human relationships. The drive to rationality in this field is the impulse to achieve equality and fellowship in the relations of persons. Any form of relation between persons which denies personal equality or which obstructs fellowship is irreligious and irrational. Indeed, in this field the two terms mean precisely the same thing. The irrationality is precisely what it is in any field, a failure to behave in terms of the real situation, in terms of the nature of the object.

RE 205

There is no inherent reason why a personal relationship should be based upon these natural functional differences. Because personal relationships are relationships of persons as persons, their functional differences have nothing directly to do with the relationship, though they may have a great deal to do with its quality and character and the ways in which it expresses itself. It is just nonsense to say that people of different races, or different professions, or different nationalities, or different sexes, cannot be friends. Of course they can, and are. Personal relationships override all the distinctions which differentiate people. Personal relationship is possible between any two persons because it is based purely on the fact that they are both persons. It may be difficult in some cases and easy in other cases. It may be fuller in some cases and more meagre in others. But it is universally possible. An Englishman may refuse to be friends with an Indian, but that is a matter of choice. It is not an impossibility. In this sense all persons are equal; and this is the first law of personal life. It does not mean that there are not immense differences between one person and another; it means that these differences have no bearing upon the possibility of personal relationships and have nothing to do with the structure or the constitution of the personal life. On the other hand, it does not mean that these differences can be ignored or should be overlooked in the personal life. The differences remain, and become the basis of the infinite variety of experience which can be shared in the life of personal relationship. When two people become friends they establish between themselves a relation of equality. They meet as equals, as man to man. There is and can be no functional subservience of one to the other. One cannot be the superior and the other the inferior. If the relation is one of inequality, then it is just not a personal relationship.

RE 103f

– 16 –

Community

Since individualism misrepresents our nature, it follows that communal life is the normal state for human beings. But human life is not organic; a shared existence is a matter of intention, not of fact. Community has to be created and sustained by conscious purpose, and the more successfully this is done the more we fulfil our personal nature.

It is a commonplace that human life is social. But like many commonplaces it is imperfectly understood, and often ignored in practice. The fact that men live normally in groups, like many of the higher animals, is of relatively little importance here. It does not touch the essence of the matter. It is not the fact that men live together that counts, but the knowledge of this fact, and the intentions to which this knowledge gives rise. What constitutes the humanity of the human group is the consciousness of each member that he belongs to it; and the intention, which pervades all his activities, to realize his membership, even if it must be, at times, in anger and revolt. It is the life of the *individual* which is a common life; and we can only be human in community. Even our secret thoughts are elements in a life that we share with our fellows; for their truth lies in their reference to a common world; and if they lose this reference they become the fancies of insanity ...

For the moment it is enough to remind ourselves that our freedom, as individuals, depends upon the co-operation of others. We are fed and clothed by our fellows. The whole apparatus of our life is provided by others. That the system of co-operation is impersonal and indirect makes it no whit less real. Nor is it merely the material resources which we use at every moment that are the gift of others. The language we speak, the thoughts we think, the ideals we cherish and pursue are only partially our own. We have them from those who went before us; and the forms they take in our private minds and mouths bear witness that they are symbols of a life that is shared.

CF 24f

A common life

It follows from this that a community cannot be brought into existence by organization. It is not functional. It is not organic. Its principle of unity is personal. It is constituted by the sharing of a common life.

It might be objected that this in itself constitutes a common purpose to which community is relative. This is a common error in contemporary civilization, and it underlies the tendency to an apotheosis of the State. It is, indeed, the erroneous postulate of any thoroughgoing individualism. It assumes that the human individual is an independent, self-contained entity with a personal life of his own which he may or may not purpose to share with others. In fact, it is the sharing of a common life which constitutes individual personality. We become persons in community, in virtue of our relations to others. Human life is *inherently* a common life. Our ability to form individual purposes is itself a function of this common life. We do indeed enter into specific relations with our fellows in virtue of specific purposes of our own; and we must do so in order to realize, in concrete experience, the *common* humanity which makes us persons. But the sharing of a common life, in general, cannot itself be a purpose. It is our nature; and in sharing a common life we are simply being ourselves by realizing our nature. Community is prior to society.

CF 56

Fellowship has to be realized in the activities of a common life, under material as well as psychological conditions which vary continually. It has to be lived through difficulties, and the difficulties have to be overcome. But provided the intention is maintained on both sides, some realization of fellowship and of freedom is certain, and some common life is necessarily established. But its quality depends upon the extent to which the fear of the other — which is the fear for the self — is overcome in practice and not merely in intention. Fellowship has to be lived: it cannot be established once for all. For though the activities of a common life may persist through habit after the intention of a fellowship has ceased, the unity which remains is no longer a fellowship but only a co-operation for common purposes.

                                                              CF 83

Any community of persons, as distinct from a mere society, is a group of individuals united in a common life, the motivation of which is positive. Like a society, a community is a group which acts together; but unlike a mere society its members are in communion with one another; they constitute a fellowship. A society whose members act together without forming a fellowship can only be constituted by a common purpose. They co-operate to achieve a purpose which each of them, in his own interest, desires to achieve, and which can only be achieved by co-operation. The relations of its members are functional; each plays his allotted part in the achievement of the common end. The society then has an organic form: it is an organization of functions; and each member is a function of the group. A community, however, is a unity of persons as persons. It cannot be defined in functional terms, by relation to a common purpose. It is not organic in structure, and cannot be constituted or maintained by organization, but only by the motives which sustain the personal relations of its members. It is constituted and maintained by a mutual affection. This can only mean that each member of the group is in positive personal relation to each of the others taken severally. The structure of a community is the nexus or network of the active relations of friendship between all possible pairs of its members.

If, then, we isolate one pair, as the unit of personal community, we can discover the basic structure of community as such. The relation between them is positively motived in each. Each, then, is heterocentric; the centre of interest and attention is in the other, not in himself. For each, therefore, it is the other who is important, not himself. The other is the centre of value. For himself he has no value in himself, but only for the other; consequently he cares for himself only for the sake of the other. But this is mutual; the other cares for him disinterestedly in return. Each, that is to say, acts, and therefore thinks and feels for the other, and not for himself. But because the positive motive contains and subordinates its negative, their unity is no fusion of selves, neither is it a functional unity of differences — neither an organic nor a mechanical unity — it is a unity of persons. Each remains a distinct individual; the other remains really other. Each realizes himself in and through the other.

Such a positive unity of persons is the self-realization of the personal. For, firstly, they are then related *as equals*. This does not mean that they have, as matter of fact, equal abilities, equal rights, equal functions or any other kind of *de facto* equality. The equality is intentional: it is an aspect of the mutuality of the relation. If it were not an equal relation, the motivation would be negative; a relation in which one was using the other as a means to his own end. Secondly, they both realize their freedom as agents, since in the absence of the fear for the self there is no constraint on either, and each can be himself fully; neither is under obligation to act a part. Thus equality and freedom are constitutive of community; and the democratic slogan, 'Liberty, equality, fraternity,' is an adequate definition of community — of the self-realization of persons in relation.

PR 157f

Religion's task is to create community. Any religion based on ideas of blood or racial kinship denies the possibility of world community, and is exclusive and potentially destructive.

Macmurray wrote the following passage during the Second World War, which he saw, in one of its aspects, as a struggle to defeat a creed which was attempting to deny the potentially universal kinship of humanity. To establish a sense of identity through race, as the Nazis did, was to ensure that other races became a threat, making war inevitable.

When we call Nazism a religion we are not using the term 'religion' in a strained or extended sense but in its most literal and exact sense. It is pathetic to find people who think that it helps to defeat Hitlerism to prove that there is no scientific basis for the theory of racial purity. We are not dealing with facts but with feelings. So long as the people concerned *feel* their 'kinship' it is of no importance whatever that its biological basis is doubtful, or even non-existent. What the religion secures is the excitement and 'sanctification' of an emotional unity of the type that is primarily derived from and referred to the natural family. The blood-relationship may be a fiction, a symbol, a myth: its effect is to produce an 'exclusive' community which distinguishes those who are 'kin' from those who are excluded, and

so turns the excluded into 'enemies.' If these excluded individuals or groups are to enter into co-operative relations with the
exclusive community, it can only be as servants or subordinates.
Thus the German racial religion can only conceive or establish
a social order in Europe on the basis of the servitude of non-
Germans.

This must suffice to illustrate what is meant by a conservative
type of religion which is concerned with the old community.
Creative religion, on the contrary, is concerned with the new
community and its creation. Like all religion its function is to
maintain an inner or emotional unity of relationship. Unlike conservative religion it is not concerned to perpetuate a community
which already exists but to achieve a community which does
not. Consequently, it must look to the future and not to the past,
as conservative religion does. To do this, it must break loose
from the hereditary, biological basis of primitive religion. It must
keep, as it were, the emotional unity which characterizes the
natural family group and yet lose its natural basis in blood-
relationship. By achieving this, it escapes from the 'exclusive'
community and becomes a 'universal' religion.

CC 38f

– 17 –

The purpose of history

Since human life is personal, and only inclusively organic, history has to be interpreted as a matter of intention rather than of evolution. It should therefore be seen as an action, *not as a* process. *Its meaning is the creation of a worldwide community in which our personal nature can be fulfilled.*

There is therefore need for a reflective discipline, the intention of which is neither to generalize nor to particularize but to record. This discipline is history, the business of which is to construct an adequate and reliable public memory. It would be wrong, or at least misleading, to say that the historian is concerned to construct the record of past events. For he is not concerned with events as such, in the scientist's sense. He does not abstract from experience a purely 'objective' world of events. He is concerned with events only as they enter into human experience, and so modify human action; only with the material world or the world of Nature so far as they provide the field of human activity and set the practical problems which men must solve. History is, then, essentially personal; and it exhibits the form of the personal: for it concentrates upon practical activities and treats the reflective achievements of an epoch as secondary and derivative; as of interest in so far as they enter into and condition the practical doings of the time. And since history is concerned with the human past in its pastness, it makes no reference to the future; it does not seek to derive from the past anything that can be referred to the future. This can be best expressed by reference to memory; for memory provides the archetypal form of all historical reflection. The ideal of history is to represent the whole human past as if it were the memory content of a single agent who had experienced it all, and whose memory was completely adequate and reliable. This ideal explains, among other things, the selectivity of history; by which I mean the way in which the representation of a past epoch varies from historian to historian and from one generation of historians to the next. This variability has led to the view that history is necessarily, and not merely accidentally, coloured by the personal prejudices and interests of the individual who writes it; and therefore is an art rather than a science, inherently subjective. In fact it is merely the 'public' form of one of the functional characteristics of memory. The 'content' of memory is not all present to consciousness at once, it is merely available when required. What requires that this or that aspect or element in memory should be recalled is always a present and practical interest. For what is actively remembered is *ipso facto* brought into a determining relation to present intentions and preoccupations. What is actually recalled is selected for its relevance to the present; and the accounts that we give of the same experience of our own from time to time necessarily vary with the occasion for their production. Nor does this variation necessarily affect their validity. Just as there can be no definitive memory, so there can be no definitive history.

As in all forms of reflection, the ideal determines the methodology of the historian. The raw material of his activity is records, that is to say, published memories. He estimates their reliability and collates them, and so builds up a composite picture which is more reliable than any of the sources taken singly. There are, of course, gaps, and these must be filled in; if possible by the discovery of further records, or if these are not available by inference and imaginative construction, which will be tested and verified in every possible fashion. The results are 'histories': themselves records to be compared and collated with the 'records' produced by other historians. So the co-operative process of reflection moves gradually in the direction of its ideal; towards a single reliable and complete record of human activity in the past, which links the past to the present in a continuity of action, and provides a public memory available to everyone.

SAA 211f

The alternatives are that we should think reality either as a unity of events or as a unity of actions; that is to say, either as one *process* or as one *action*.

Contemporary thought, under the dominant influence of science, does, at least implicitly, conceive the world as a single process; either biologically as an evolutionary process, or mathematically as a material process of events obeying physical laws.

But we are in a position to reject this alternative decisively. For we have seen that the conception of a unity of events, whether conceived physically or organically, is the conception of the continuant, and that the continuant is an ideal abstraction from our experience as agents. It is constituted by the exclusion of action. This concept of process cannot therefore include action as an element in the unity it seeks to express. If the world is a unitary process, it must be a world in which nothing is ever done; in which everything simply happens; a world, then, in which everything is matter of fact and nothing is ever intended. We should have to assert, in that case, that there are no actions; that what seem such are really events. It will not be sufficient to say that all our actions are determined; for this is a contradiction in terms. The capacity to act is freedom; what has to be denied, if the world is one event, is that anything is ever intended. But in that case the assertion itself must be unintentional, and therefore meaningless. In rejecting this alternative, we are merely using the criterion that we established earlier, that since the 'I do' is the primary certainty, any theory which explicitly or implicitly denies it must be false.

SAA 219

History is intentional

We must, therefore, as agents, think the world as a unity: and we have seen that this unity can only be coherently thought as a unity of action. This means that we must think the world in which we act, and of which we are constituents, as a unity of intention. But, admittedly, any thought, however formal, requires verification, and the possibility of verification is grounded on the differential effect it has upon intention. If we act as if the world, in its unity, is intentional; that is, if we believe in practice that the world is one action — and our consideration of history has shown us what this signifies — we shall act differently from anyone who does not believe this. We shall act as though our own actions were our contributions to the one conclusive action which is the history of the world. If, on the other hand, we believe that the world is a mere process of events which happen as they happen, we shall act differently. Our conception of the unity of the world determines a way of life; and the satis-

factoriness or unsatisfactoriness of that way of life is its verification.

The heart of this verification must lie in the effect of the belief
upon the relations of persons; and only when we have considered this topic will it be possible to go beyond the formality
of our present conclusion. Meanwhile, in bringing to a close the
first stage of our inquiry, we may profitably return to our
starting-point. The long argument of modern philosophy, we
said, has moved steadily in the direction of an atheistic conclusion; and with it the historical development of our civilization
has moved towards irreligion. At the same time this has pre-
cipitated a revolutionary crisis in society, and made a break in
the philosophical tradition which compels us to start afresh from
a revision of its fundamental assumption, the primacy of the
theoretical. We have substituted the 'I do' for the 'I think,' and
made a first tentative effort to follow out the implications of this
radical modification. Very much remains obscure; but there is
one result which is sufficiently clear. The argument which starts
from the primacy of the practical moves steadily in the direction
of a belief in God. To think the world in practical terms is
ultimately to think the unity of the world as one action, and
therefore as informed by a unifying intention.

It may, indeed, prove possible to think the process of the
world as intentional without thinking a supreme Agent whose
act the world is. But *prima facie,* at least, it is not possible to do
so. The conflict between religion and atheism turns, in large part
at least, on the issue whether the process of the world is
intentional or not. We noticed, in our first chapter, that contemporary existentialism, in its division into theist and atheist
wings, poses the substantial problem of philosophy in our day
in the alternatives, 'God or Nothing.' We may now add to this,
as a pointer to the direction of a verification, that the theistic
alternative issues in the hope of an ultimate unity of persons in
fellowship, which gives meaning to human effort; while atheist
existentialism finds human relationship an insoluble problem
and all human projects doomed to frustration and ultimate
meaninglessness. As Sartre says in *Huis clos,* 'L'enfer, c'est les
autres.'

SAA 220–22

– 18 –

Greeks, Romans and Hebrews

Macmurray suggested that in order to understand European history we need to look at the three cultures which have dominated it. In his view, each of these cultures corresponds to one of the unity-patterns. Rome, with its emphasis on law and administration, was predominantly mechanical in its values; Greece, predominantly aesthetic, corresponds to the organic pattern; and the Hebrew tradition, based on religion and on the idea of a God who relates to humans and acts in history, embodied the personal. European history is the story of the tension between these different influences, and much of our trouble, according to Macmurray, stems from the particular dominance of the Roman outlook.

Three old civilizations have been mixed together to form the culture of which we are the heirs — the Hebrew, the Greek and the Roman, a religious, an artistic and an organizing, administrative or scientific civilization. These three streams of old experience have never really fused. Indeed the main problem of European civilization hitherto has arisen from the strain that their antagonisms have set up, and from the effort, never successful, to unite them in a single culture.

The dominant influence in our civilization has been the influence of the Roman Empire. The Romans were deficient on the artistic and on the religious side. They adopted the Greek culture, and then the Christian religion, when they found that mere organization and administrative efficiency could not serve to maintain the unity of the Empire. But they accepted them as tributaries and servants of imperialism, while despising profoundly both Greeks and Christians. Greek art they found useful to adorn the leisure of the educated classes, and Christianity as 'dope' for the masses, to distract them from thoughts of revolution. To this day our culture has remained in that Roman mould. It is essentially imperialist; that is to say, its governing ideal is the maintenance and perfecting of an efficient organization of social life, depending on law, industrial management and the maintenance of power for the defence of law and property. Art and religion have been harnessed to the service of this ideal of administrative and organizing efficiency and subordinated to it. We are proud of Shakespeare and our artistic achievements — especially when they are a century or more in the past — but we look upon the artist and his artistic temperament as queer and disorderly and a little contemptible. We are annoyed with anyone who dares to deny that we are Christians, but at the same time we are inclined to look upon the pious saint as a nuisance and a mollycoddle. Such is the immense power of persistence of the tradition of the Roman Empire! We are Romans at heart, even in our extremes of Fascism and Communism, though like the Romans we are willing to use art and religion so long as they agree to play the part of menials to our ideal of social efficiency.

FMW 74–76

The pragmatic consciousness finds its clearest historical expression in Ancient Rome, the contemplative in Ancient Greece. The religious consciousness has its only effective historical expression in the Ancient Hebrews. The difference between the pragmatic and the contemplative consciousness is the difference between the Romans and the Greeks. That difference has been defined for us by scholars and historians again and again. The characteristic achievements of the Romans are technical achievements. They are feats of organization, administration and engineering. The Romans, we say, were an intensely practical people. This way of expressing it conveys a precise meaning. The habit of the Roman mind makes it see life in terms of practical problems to be solved, and it sets itself to the invention of solutions. When the Roman mind sets to work in the field of art, it reveals consciousness of its own inadequacy by imitating Greek models.

CH 21

For the Greek thinkers, therefore, the very idea of change is excluded from the essence of the divine; and the life of God is a life of eternally changeless contemplation of the eternally changeless. In this we see the apotheosis of leisure — the ideal of aristocracy. God is the opposite of a worker. The dualism of theory and practice rejects practice and idealizes the theoretical life. To this ideal human life can only approximate even at its best. The element of evil in the world, which frustrates all efforts to achieve complete stability, makes it impossible even for the most fortunate and gifted of aristocrats to escape from the necessities of the practical life. The social meaning of this ideal finds its classical expression in the *Republic* of Plato. In that fairest and falsest of all Utopias we have a record of the most uncompromising effort to imagine a perfect society on the assumption that perfection means changelessness.

CH 109

The contrast between the Greek and Roman social achievements is a contrast of opposites at the same level. Both are dualist societies, subject to the opposition of spiritual and material ideals. The Greek sacrifices the material to the spiritual; the Roman sacrifices the spiritual to the material. In the social field this means that the Greek clings to the natural community of which the family is the type, in which the bonds of unity are spiritual bonds, based upon personal intercourse and direct co-operation. But he can only achieve this in a very small community which defends itself against the rest of mankind by an intense exclusiveness and conservatism. He has to sacrifice universality to emotional unity. The Roman, on the other hand, sacrifices inner unity to universality, and achieves an empire based upon the external pressure of law and administration, backed by force. Each is destroyed by what it has excluded — the Greek world by its incapacity to combine into a larger national group; the Roman by the lack of cultural cohesion.

CH 112

The development of the primitive group towards civilization inevitably dissociates the two bases of unity, so that they no longer define the same group. For this effect, the institution of slavery is decisive. In any slave-owning society the spiritual unity of fellowship is limited to a part of the co-operating group. The slaves are included in the society as co-operating members; they are excluded from the community of fellowship. From this point onwards it is rare to find a society in which both principles of unity define the same group of persons. The institution of an agricultural economy, and the settled life that goes with it, introduces territorial boundaries, and gives an impetus to the growth of property, and particularly of property in land. In consequence, residence within the territory of the group appears as a qualification for membership, and ownership of land within its boundaries is a qualification for *full* membership of the community. The development of trade between independent territorial groups complicates and diversifies both types of unity. Co-operation passes beyond the limits of territorial and so of legal control; and some members of the group are linked in friendship with strangers. This process is well exemplified in the history of ancient Greece, and it produced the situation which created the imperialism first of Macedon and then of Rome: and in the city states of Greece, as in Hitler's Germany, it gave rise to the reactionary ideal of 'self-sufficiency' — the vain effort to re-establish the primitive coincidence of co-operation and fellowship within the territorial limits of political independence.

In the Roman Empire the attempt to combine the two principles of unity has been given up. Its unity is a unity of organized co-operation within which religious and cultural toleration allows older unities of fellowship to maintain themselves and new forms of fellowship to develop autonomously. The Romans created in this way the modern idea of the State, as a unity of society based wholly upon law and administration, and so providing a framework within which co-operation can be organized and developed. The State, so conceived and constructed, has a pragmatic justification only. It is not concerned with culture, with unities of fellowship, except in so far as they threaten to disrupt the system of co-operation which it maintains. Its business in this field is the negative one of 'keeping the peace.'

Within such a system of administration, provided it is efficient, there tends to grow up a sentiment of loyalty to the institutions it maintains, and a sense of unity with all one's fellow-citizens. This inner shadow of the external system of co-operation is real enough, and can under suitable circumstances and by suitable methods provide a strong motive for common action. But since it is impersonal in its nature, and dependent upon self-interest in the efficiency of the system of government, it has not the binding force of a sense of fellowship which is direct and personal. In the history of the Roman Empire, therefore, we find attempts to strengthen its inner unity by appeals to religion; first, in the deification of Rome, and of the Emperor as the personal symbol of Rome; and finally by the adoption of Christianity as the official religion of Rome. So there was created, in the society of the Roman Empire, what has remained the ideal pattern of social unity for West European civilization. The two principles of human unity are recognized as functionally separate. Church and State are charged with the care of the inner and the outer unity of society respectively.

In this final phase of the history of the Roman Empire the external, territorial, legal unity is already realized. The task of the Church is, as it were, to transform the unity of co-operation into a unity of fellowship. After the collapse of the Roman Empire the situation was reversed. The Church survived the State, and it fell to the Church to create the unity of Western civilization anew, with the ideal inherited from the Roman Empire as its guiding principle. In this case it was the spiritual unification of western Europe which came first. What was created was Christendom — an inner unity of fellowship through a common religion. The task which remained was to create a corresponding political and administrative framework for Christendom so that it might be also an effective co-operative unity. This political unification of Europe was never effectively realized. The Holy Roman Empire remained a form and a hope which failed to achieve substance. When the medieval world gave way to the modern, the new, protestant forms of religion shrank within the framework of the new independent states and modern nationalism was born.

CF 62–65

Macmurray reserved his greatest admiration for the Hebrew achievement. Against the dominance of the law, the prophets insisted on the personal nature of morality and religious observance. Their insights were fulfilled in the life and teachings of Jesus. The impetus behind the Christian Church, despite all its corruptions and failings, is to create an inclusive community which will recognize the equality of all human beings. This equality, which transcends racial and cultural differences, is rooted in the personal nature of humans, and in their relationship to God.

The central difficulty is perhaps to unite and hold together the personality and the universality in the religious conception. The cleavage between the priestly conception and the prophetic conception of religion in the Old Testament is a good example of this, and ready to our hand. The priestly type is predominantly practical and ethical. Its effort is to unify all activities under the law which expresses the will of God for man. If this can be done, then in the field of practice the universality that is demanded has been achieved. Life has been brought into subjection to God. This is indeed less than is requisite even in the practical field, since nature as well as human life must be uniformly and together dominated by the one law, a fact which explains why the priestly type of religion invariably connects the keeping of the law with material prosperity. Human life perfectly submitted to the will of God could not be out of harmony with a Nature which is the creature of the same divine purpose.

The defect of the priestly type of religion is this. The more it succeeds in its task of subjecting all life to the divine law, the more completely it drives personality from the field, and the less spiritual does it become. This is the brunt of the attack upon it made by the great prophets, by Christ and by Paul. In becoming a practical and detailed law, imposed on men, it becomes external, mechanical and unspiritual. Morality becomes a conformity, conformity to an ever-increasing, all-pervading system of regulation in which the freedom and spontaneity of the personal life is choked. The spirit finds itself in bondage. Three specific indictments of the legal religion may be mentioned. There is first the theme of the book of Job. All empirical justification is lacking for the belief that obedience to the divine law is crowned by material prosperity. A hiatus appears between the law that governs the holy life and the law that governs nature. There is, secondly, the attack of the apostle Paul. The exacting demands of the divine law cannot be realized in the lives of sinful men. Its effect can only be to isolate men from God and so make a life of fellowship with God impossible. Christ's attack on Pharisaism goes deeper than either, to the root of the matter. 'The Sabbath is made for man, not man for the Sabbath.' In spite of the possibility which it opens up of a universality of divine control, the legal religion is fundamentally unspiritual. It subordinates personality to an external control, and in this implicitly denies the spiritual life. Under the law life becomes 'play-acting,' a sham fight in which acts of duty have ceased to be the expression of spiritual quality. Such a universal control of life by an external authority which, like the modern universality of science, nullifies personality, cannot express the nature of God, for God is personal.

Thus the priestly type of religious development, seeking a

short cut to the subordination of all things to God, fails signally. In its religious fervour for universality it sacrifices personality. It ceases to be religion, fails even to be a morality, and becomes merely law, an imposition upon the spiritual life which must destroy it in proportion to the success with which it achieves its object. Such a conception of religion can have no objectivity. Even could human life be successfully subordinated to the law, what proof could there be that this law was in fact what it claimed to be, the absolute expression of the divine will? The only conceivable form of proof would be that which the Stoic philosophers sought, its conformity to the law of nature. But any such appeal could only discover its origins in human tradition, and so convict it of complete subjectivity.

The prophetic type of religious development stands in strong contrast to this. It is a personal religion in two senses. It has its being in the spiritual experience of individual men, rooted in their insight into spiritual qualities and spiritual relations, and its central theme is the nature of the divine personality. On this side the Old Testament tells the story of a steady growth of spiritual insight into the character of God, which rests upon the inner conflicts of a long succession of spiritually minded men. Each prophet stands, as it were, on his own experience, and builds upon it his own conviction of the character of God. We should remember here that 'personal' experience is not mere 'individual' experience. It is largely the experience of other men, predecessors and contemporaries, built into the structure of a man's own being, fused with himself and cast in an individual mould. This alone makes possible a spiritual development through the generations of a people's history, and creates a community of spiritual belief. In its general character this growing body of prophetic religion is an interpretation of the divine personality in terms of an experience of the human.

A 195–98

The reference to Rome is not out of place. Even if we did not have the story of the three temptations, we should have been certain that one of the subjects which he pondered in the wilderness was the Roman empire and the place of Israel in it. Without this he could not have stood within the tradition of the Hebrew prophets. And even though one were to think him in error in claiming to be the Messiah, one could not deny that he was one of the great Hebrew prophets. I cannot but assume that before he launched his mission he must have convinced himself that he was 'He that should come.' This is another question that we can be sure he thought over in the wilderness.

Knowing the situation he faced, we can make a fair guess at the issues that he thought over. His people, the chosen people of God, were now tributary subjects in the empire of Augustus. The Roman ascendancy, however, was fairly recent. It had brought to a close more than a century of struggles for freedom, beginning with the revolt of the Maccabees against the effort of the King of Syria to force pagan religion upon Judaea. Its success in its immediate object was followed by struggles for national independence. These, too, had temporary successes. But internal struggles for power led eventually to an appeal to the Romans, the siege of Jerusalem by Pompey and the annexation of Palestine in 65 BC, But the memory of the struggle was still alive, and attempts to throw off the Roman yoke were made, which came to nothing. If Jesus were to claim to be the Messiah, he would be expected by many Jews, perhaps a majority, to renew the military struggle. On this issue, he had to make a clear decision. His answer, as we have seen, was a decisive 'No.' The reason, stated later, was that 'they that take the sword shall perish with the sword.' To worship Satan by taking up the sword could result, even if its success were total, only in the founding of a Jewish empire on the Roman model. The kingdom of heaven could only be built on wholly different principles.

Jesus could well maintain that God, in his purpose to restore the kingdom of heaven on earth, had permitted the establishment of the Roman empire. 'Caesar has established justice, security and peace,' he might say, 'over a great number of nations, and holds them together in a far-spread unity. Within it we Jews are free to live, within the empire, by the principles of human community revealed to us. This then is our task. If we take up arms and win, we may gain the whole world, but we shall lose our own soul in the process. A true community cannot be established by force, only by consent. The tribute is a small price to pay to Caesar for the benefits he bestows. The only proper course is to live the true life of human community in the Roman empire and to transform it from within.'

PJ 5f

A religion which rests upon a limited and exclusive basis, such as family or nationality or race, though it demands and tends to sustain brotherhood and equality within the exclusive circle, fosters a sentiment of difference and inequality in all relationships which cross its boundaries. Only a religion which looks to a universal community contains the principle of democracy in all political relations as a necessary implication. A religion, such as Christianity, which does envisage a universal community — the brotherhood of man — is also incompatible with any political organization which is not, in the essential and effective sense, democratic.

But it is not necessary to argue that Christianity *implies* democracy. Already the implication is discovered and emphasized in the New Testament, in no uncertain terms. When Jesus conceived and confronted the task of transforming the political universality of the Roman Empire into the theocratic community of the Kingdom of Heaven, he chose his instruments from the common people, and taught them, in precept and parable and example, to base their relationships upon the mutual service of equals and to condemn and exclude the desire for power. 'He that would be greatest among you,' he said, 'let him be the servant of all.' Explicitly he contrasts with this principle of democratic community the practice of the kings of the nations who exercise authority over their subjects. In particular he insists upon *economic* democracy. His gospel is for the poor and it is 'easier for a camel to go through the needle's eye than for a rich man to enter the kingdom of God.' St Paul formulates the inherent democracy of the gospel when he asserts that God has chosen the weak things of the world to confound the mighty. It is no accident that the *Magnificat* has held such a place through the centuries in the liturgies of the Churches. For its thanksgiving to a God who puts down the mighty from their seats and exalts the humble and meek, comes from the inmost heart of Christianity. Perhaps the statement which comes nearest to the sentiment of the modern democrat is that one which says, 'Call no man master, for one is your master, even Christ, and all ye are brethren.'

CC 44f

After the death of Jesus, the small body of disciples who remained faithful to his intention and who proceeded to carry on his mission was a Jewish group, and the tendency to look upon itself as a Jewish sect was the cause of the earliest debates in the Christian community. But this reactionary tendency was quickly overcome, and the true understanding of their mission prevailed. The missionary journeys of St Paul had the effect of making the new movement in fact, as well as in intention, international. It cannot have been long before the non-Jewish Christians in the Roman Empire out-numbered the Jewish Christians. It would seem that St Paul deliberately aimed at establishing a Christian community in Rome itself, at the centre of the Empire, and the character and the length of his Epistle to the Romans bears witness to the importance which this church had in his eyes, at the strategic centre of the Roman world. Yet it is in this epistle that he rejects most eloquently any tendency to belittle the importance of the Jewish origin of the gospel and of the continuity of the Hebrew culture with the new Christian movement. For some time, no doubt, the primacy of the mother church in Jerusalem was recognized; but the destruction of Jerusalem by Titus in AD 70 must have put an end to any lingering tendency to look upon Palestine as the natural home of Christians and Jews alike. Half a century after the death of Jesus Christianity was already a scattered community of men and women mainly from the lower classes, permeating the Roman Empire, predominantly non-Jewish, recognizing no barriers of nationality, race or class, waiting for the destruction of the Roman Empire and the establishing of the kingdom of heaven in its place, and seeking meanwhile to live communally in accordance with the principles of the kingdom as Jesus had expounded them. The first stage of the permeation of Europe by Christianity had begun, with Rome as its centre.

CH 122f

– 19 –

The dangers of idealism

We have seen that Macmurray regarded idealism as a dangerous illu-
sion (see Chapter 1). We have also seen that, in contrast to Marx, he
did not identify idealism with religion. In a wartime lecture, he
explained why he held these views. For Macmurray, the Hebrews were
a unique example of a religious culture, free from any taint of idealism.
If religion were not to be destroyed, it must be rescued from idealism,
and its true nature made clear. This issue is fundamental to an under-
standing of Macmurray's thought.

... it is my belief that religion and idealism are enemies, and at
war with one another: that idealism is a disease of the spirit
which infects its marrow, and as it spreads it blinds us to the
reality of the religious life, and shuts us up in the world of our
sick fantasies. The disease has had a long course; in our time it
has reached its climax. Our Christianity is very sick, and cannot
recover until it is cured of idealism.

I should not be surprised if this should seem an extraordinary, and even a perverse statement to make. For to many
people idealism seems to be the very soul of religion, and to
attack idealism appears to be to make war on religion itself. Is
not religion the mainstay of our ideals? Is not its function to
implant, sustain and energize them? We praise religious
idealism, but who has ever heard of a religious crusade against
idealism? I am well aware that for most religious people in our
time, idealism and religion are identical, or at least closely
linked together. But in our time also religion is in decline, and
I suggest that these two things are not unrelated. The belief that
religion and idealism are identical is the cardinal mistake of our
contemporary civilization, both among the friends and the
enemies of religion ...

... There was one man of genius in the last century who based
his whole system of thought on the identification of religion and
idealism. He was Karl Marx; and to-day his devoted followers

are counted in millions. It was because Marx identified religion and idealism that he decided that religion must be abolished. The radical atheism of the communist movement is rooted in the conviction that religion is inherently and essentially idealist, and the most potent influence in human life for establishing and popularizing idealism. I believe that the communists are wrong in this and that the Marxian critique of religion, which Marx thought the basis of all social criticism, is mistaken. If he had been right, I should have agreed with him that religion must be fought and destroyed.

IAR 6f

. If I am to explain myself, I must clearly begin by indicating what I mean by idealism. Someone is sure to wish to know whether I am using the term in the philosophical or in the popular sense. I shall begin therefore by saying that I mean both, since the one is the reflective and elaborated form of the other. Philosophical idealism, of which the Hegelian tradition is the most influential form in modern times, provides a logical basis, and a metaphysical formulation of the idealism of popular speech and thought and outlook. Philosophy is always related, when it is alive and not merely archaeological, to the unreflective culture of its time and its society. The only qualification which I feel called upon to make, is this: that the language of idealism has become so widespread that it is used at times, for want of any other, by those who mean something else; and then it tends to mislead and bewilder those who use it.

The essence of idealism whether in its popular or in its philosophical form, lies in an emotional attachment to ideas rather than to things. Since the emotional life contains the springs of action, this means that those activities of human life which are concerned with ideas are preferred over those which are concerned with material objects, and are undertaken, encouraged and valued *for their own sake*. From this root idealism spreads its branches through every department of individual and social life; and in accepting it, religion confirms and sanctifies it. The religious life becomes the life which turns away from material things to occupy itself with the things of the soul. The real life of a man becomes the life of the mind, the life of thought and contemplation.

This, then, is what I mean by idealism, and what I count as

the radical error of our civilization. It may be well, therefore, before we consider its implications and its effects, to indicate at once, right at the source, why it is wrong. To do this, we need only consider the relation between things and ideas. Ideas are, ideas *of* things. They are 'about' things. They *refer* to things. It is by having ideas that we know things, that we can have opinions and beliefs about the world. Ideas are our own creatures, we form them in our minds. Things exist in their own right, independently of us, in the world. Our ideas may be true or false; and if we ask what makes them true or false, the answer must be the actual nature of the things to which they refer. The value of an idea lies in its truth; and its truth depends, not upon itself, but upon the thing it is about and to which it refers. These are not the conclusions of some special philosophy, but the starting points of all philosophy, the elements of common knowledge and common sense. Things are primary. They stand on their own feet, and are what they are. Ideas are secondary. They are for the sake of things; they *mean* things; and their function is to enable us to get at things and to know and understand them.

Now if we become emotionally attached to ideas, and value them for their own sake we break the relation between ideas and things. We treat them as independent of the things to which they refer. They become valuable in themselves, not as a means for getting effectively in touch with things. In their proper nature ideas are mediators between ourselves and reality. We go through them to the things they represent. But if we transfer our interest and our affection to ideas, then we stop short at the ideas and go no farther. They become like stained-glass windows which we look at and do not look through. We become shut up in our own minds, shut away from real things, and the life of the mind spends itself in manipulating its ideas so that they are good and satisfying to look at; instead of arranging them so that they are easier to see through. Truth is lost, or becomes, at best, accidental, since truth depends upon the relation of ideas to things, and we no longer are concerned with this relation, but only with the relation of ideas to ideas. Knowledge becomes impossible, for knowledge is of things and is only to be had by those who are interested in things. We are left with the lovely traceries and patterns that thought weaves, and begin to imagine that this beauty is truth. But it is not, it is only what it comforts us and satisfies us to believe.

The first consequence of idealism is that it institutes a dualism which splits the world in two. When ideas are valued in their relation to things there is no break in the unity of the world for us. But if we value ideas for themselves they are separated from things and form a world of their own. So we find ourselves with two worlds for one; a world of things and a world of ideas; a spiritual world and a material world. We have to deal with both and live in both; so we acquire two lives; an inner life and an outer life; a life of the body and a life of the mind; a material life and a spiritual life. The one is concerned with physical things; the other with ideal things, things not of the world in which we toil and suffer, fail and sin. There is this world and another world; this life and another life. When idealism makes conquest of religion, religion becomes concerned with the other life, the spiritual life; and with the other world which is so different from this. Thus when we fall a prey to idealism we distinguish the material from the spiritual, and set them in opposition; and the root of this is that we value ideas above things; so that instead of recognizing that ideas are about things, we behave as if things were about ideas; and our religion begins to treat this world as if it were for the sake of the other, and referred to it. So we invert the natural order.

The power of the mind to form and to arrange ideas is the imagination. If ideas then are separated from things and accepted for themselves, they are imaginary. This other, ideal world is necessarily a world of fancy, an imaginary world. The structure of it is the work of phantasy. This does not mean that it is pure day-dreaming, in which anything may happen. That is only the raw material of the imagination. The working of the mind upon it has its own laws of creative activity, and at its highest the product of this activity is a work of art. It has its own unity and its own standards. But in this artistry the imagination is not bound by the facts; it is free of the world of actual, material existence. Consequently, the ideal world has its standards in our own demands. It is constructed to satisfy us; and since one of our deepest demands is for community, it will not satisfy us completely unless it satisfies also those whom we love and respect. In the end — and that is in the demand for total community, which is a demand of our religious nature — it must satisfy all men, and have a universal validity. So religious idealism seeks to construct, in imagination, a world which satisfies all the demands of the human spirit. This is the ideal world, the heaven for which we long and in which we would be fully satisfied; the phantasy world of all mankind.

But the actual world in which we have to live, and which we know — the material world of things — is different. Our knowledge of it is a structure of ideas, of course, built by the same power of the imagination; but it is everywhere bound by the facts and is built to represent and to refer to things as they actually are. And things as they are do not satisfy us wholly. Often we would wish them to be otherwise. There is evil and suffering in the actual world, and the necessity for incessant labour and weariness. There is the necessity of growing old, with death at the end of the road. There is the need to deal with people who are not much concerned with our satisfaction, and who hurt us in their eagerness for their own. Consequently it must contrast strongly with any ideal world which is constructed to be satisfactory to us. The ideal world is always, for this reason, a better world; a world of things as they ought to be, in which people behave as they ought to behave; where poverty and suffering and evil and death have no place. The two worlds which are generated by the separation of things and ideas are different in quality. The ideal world is better than the actual; the spiritual world is more satisfying than the material. So the ideal world becomes the standard for the actual; the actual world is judged by the ideal; and the standards of behaviour in the ideal world become the measure of how we ought to behave; and determine the moral ideal. The ideal way of behaving stands in contrast to the way we actually behave.

Religious idealism completes this process by achieving belief in this ideal world. We believe in the other world when we assert that it, and not the actual world, is the real world. Idealist philosophy sets itself the task to prove this, and maintains that the Real is the Ideal. And since the two worlds stand in contrast, if we believe in the ideal world, we do not believe in the actual world. Now it is just here that the crux of the situation is reached. For willy-nilly, whatever we believe, we have to live in the actual world. Consequently we *know* that this world is the real one; and into our belief in the other there always enters an element of self-deception. The belief is always a somewhat imaginary belief. The convinced idealist, who believes that he will enter the other world, and live in it after death, rarely shows any more eagerness to be done with this life than the out-and-out materialist. Often, indeed, he shows more reluctance to risk his life than the unbeliever. Action is the acid test of real belief; and the real significance of idealism, as the sincere religious idealist will at once admit, is the effect that it has upon action in this world. What then is the practical effect of idealism?

For the idealist, the business of life in this world must be the realization of ideals. This can be considered from many angles, and leads to quite diverse conceptions of the good life; the clash of which creates religious controversy and dissension. But we need not consider the ambiguities which arise and I shall limit myself to the one which is most prominent in our minds to-day, the realization of a better order of life in the world after this war. The point I wish to make is independent of the particular way in which we seek the realization of ideals; it is common to them all. It is that it must always involve self-deception.

An ideal is something contrasted with what is actual; something that we think would be better than what actually exists or happens. To realize an ideal means to change the world, and make it like the ideal. The ideal is to be used as a standard or a criterion which determines our action; as a blueprint of a better world. The way to realize our ideal world, is to act in such a way that the actual world will be transformed into the likeness of the ideal. But this is impossible; because the ideal world is a different world from the one in which we must act. It is not built in reference to the world of fact, but for the satisfaction of ourselves. It has never taken into consideration the conditions of action in the material world, where it is only possible to act successfully in terms of what its nature allows. A man may have the highest ideals, but they do not begin to tell him how they are to be realized; for that an entirely different outlook on the world is necessary, and a knowledge of the world, not of the ideal. When the idealist turns from the contemplation of the ideal to action he is in the material world and has turned away from the other world — the world of ideas. He must deal now with facts, with what refuses to satisfy him; with a world of things, and of people who have ways of their own and insist on going *their* way and not *his*. He must behave, if he is to act at all, in a way that satisfies the facts. He cannot, if he would, act in the real world as if it were the ideal world; he must leave that other world behind him. For, as we saw, it is of the essence of the ideal that it has lost its reference to the actual. That is how it arises. What then can he do to realize his ideal? He can hold on to his ideal on the one hand, as the hope of the future. He can do what seems best in the circumstances, and hope that the result will move in the direction of the ideal which he cherishes. But it is a blind hope and a vain hope. It is blind, because the ideal is a stained-glass window which gives no view of what exists outside it. It is vain because when he goes out of his cathedral into the outside world he must act as men act in the real world, in a way and by principles which are different from those of the ideal world; and consequently the result must be different too. Indeed he himself belongs to both worlds, and is divided against himself. His actual motives are different from his ideal motives; and his actual motives are the motives from which his actual conduct flows. His idea of himself has no reference to the man he actually is. He cannot know himself; his idealism makes that impossible. So he must constantly think that he is doing one thing (the ideal thing) from one motive (the ideal motive) when in material fact he is doing another thing from another motive. Idealism always involves self-deception; a perfect idealism would involve complete self-deception. If we attach our emotional life to the world of ideas, we do not merely separate the ideas from the material world. We separate the material world from ideas, and leave it to run its own course by its own automatism; and action conforms to the fashion of this present world. It proceeds by habit and by tradition. So when the idealist faces the need for social change, he becomes passionately interested in the idea of building a better world; but he is not interested in building it. He believes he is, because his mind is full of it. But his hands are not.

This then is my case against idealism. Yet even if you were to agree with me, I fancy you might still think that it was a case against religion. I have still to explain why I refuse this identification of religion and idealism, and insist that idealism is against religion, and that religion is destroyed by it.

IAR 8–17

God in this world

To escape from idealism religion must recover its reference to the actuality of this world, and to the immediacy of the present as the point of action in this life. If it were cured of idealism, religion would be about this world, and not about any other world. Its beliefs would provide an interpretation of the common life of humanity, and would find their evidence in history and common experience; not in special experiences and strange visions. More than this, its beliefs would be drawn *from* experience; they would arise in our contact with fact, and they would grow with the growth of experience and be tested and retested and remade as experience demanded. They would not be fixed, dogmatic or authoritarian. Instead of thinking about religious things, we should think ordinary things in a religious way. Instead of living a spiritual life which is separate from and in opposition to our material life we should live our ordinary life spiritually. Instead of believing in the idea of God, we should seek and find God in this world — a God who does not depend on us and our believings or disbelievings, but on whom we depend. Our religion would cease to be for our comfort or consolation, a compensation for the futilities and failure of our material life, and become power and knowledge for the salvation of the world through us, and even at our expense.

IAR 18f

But the life of the mind, without its intentional relation to the life of personal community, is the isolation of the individual, and the disintegration of community. To substitute the idea of personal unity for the fact of it is to deny community. For the life of the imagination is necessarily solitary; and the world of ideas is a private world. The life of community can only be lived in action, for only in the material world can we meet; and only action can be common. It is indeed easy, in exalted mood, to retire into the solitariness of one's own spirit, and there to feel the warmest affection for all mankind, and to be at one with our fellows. For thus the will is quiescent, and the emotions are attached to the idea of community. But the experience is inherently deceptive; for the reference to material fact is lost; the actual people with whom we must come to grips in action, whose wills are other than our own, whose desires oppose our own, and who frustrate, by their misguided obstinacy and wrongheadedness, or by their selfishness and cruelty, our best efforts after peace and fellowship, are out of the picture, or idealized by the alchemy of imagination. To cherish our ideas and ideals is a form of self-love, even if what we cherish is our idea of other people. Our idea of others is our own; and is shaped to our satisfaction. They themselves are not ours, but in very truth other than us; and their existence is a continuous challenge to us, to our ideas, and to our ideals. Community cannot be realized in idea; for its realization involves the subordination of the self and its ideas to the interests and needs of others. Idealist religion makes the realization of community impossible by its preoccupation with the idea of a universal community and of its realization. For by attaching our emotions to the idea it withdraws the motives of action from the field of action; and cutting the idea from its reference, it blinds us to the actuality of the world in which our action must operate. The task of religion is to co-operate with God in the creation of the true community, of the kingdom of heaven on earth, which is His creative act in history. Idealism can only blind and paralyse us in the face of this task.

IAR 21f

– 20 –

Faith

The idea of faith is often travestied as being a fixed, irrational belief in some improbable and unverifiable set of ideas. Macmurray, however, saw faith as an attitude of mind essential to scientific investigation, and argued that there are similarities between scientific and religious faith.

In this description of knowledge it is possible to recognize the element of faith. Faith makes its appearance the moment a deliberate activity is insisted upon as an essential element in the process of knowledge. I do *not* mean that the scientist substitutes for certainty in his beliefs any sort of instinctive conviction that they are right. That is not faith but superstition. I mean that while recognizing that his beliefs are only probable he does not throw up the sponge. He trusts to activity to procure him the means for their modification. He is willing to act upon the basis of beliefs which he knows to be uncertain, but which themselves have been tested up to a point. This is faith, and it is now clear that faith is an attitude of will rather than of reason; a question of what you propose to *do* in face of your ignorance. Speculative reason is grounded in practical reason, as Kant held. Knowledge rests upon the will to know, and has its ultimate origin in a moral demand. This is expressed precisely in the definition of faith given in the Epistle to the Hebrews (I quote from Moffat's translation), 'Faith means we are confident *of what we hope for*: convinced *of what we do not see.*' What the scientist hopes for is not to prove that he is right. He hopes for greater knowledge. This implies a critical attitude to his own beliefs. It involves also certain demands which he makes of the universe. If he is to experiment he must believe that there is something which he does not know; that this something is a regularity or principle involved in the facts he is observing; and that by taking the right steps, by thought and imagination, by observation and appropriate activity, he can discover it. These demands are postulates of his scientific practice. We might paraphrase another verse of the same chapter, and say, 'Without faith it is impossible to gain knowledge; for he that would know must believe that the world is knowable and that it does discover knowledge to him that seeks it.' Such an attitude does away with dogma, because it recognizes that all knowledge is only partial. Equally it does away with scepticism, because it proposes to live and grow by the knowledge which it has, however uncertain. It is an attitude of mind at once thoroughly critical and thoroughly confident.

A 36f

After analysing how the word 'faith' is used in the Gospels, Macmurray concluded that it does not mean belief in a set of intellectual propositions. Christ contrasts 'faith' with 'fear.' Faith is an emotional principle of evaluation which enables us to live fully and courageously.

A cursory examination of the Gospels is sufficient to make it clear that Christ's own use of the term 'faith' does not allow us to take it as the equivalent of 'belief' in the ordinary sense of holding certain views. Very frequently the term is used without qualification of any kind to describe a certain practical attitude of mind which is the condition of some unusual achievement. It appears to be a quality of personality which is normally more conspicuous by its absence than by its presence. 'How is it that ye have no faith?' 'If ye have faith as a grain of mustard-seed, ye shall say to this mountain, "Be thou removed, and be thou cast into the sea, and it shall be done".' Here obviously faith does not mean believing something, nor is it even qualified by a reference to an object believed in or to a person trusted. It is not faith about something, nor faith in some one, but simply faith, some inherent quality, as it were, in the mind; perhaps a general readiness to trust, an absence of hesitation and of the reckoning of consequences, as defined in the injunction, 'Take therefore no thought for the morrow ... Sufficient unto the day is the evil thereof.'

The meaning of the term grows clearer if we examine certain other terms with which it is commonly connected. In the recorded sayings of Christ faith is characteristically contrasted with fear. 'Why are ye so fearful?' He says to His disciples, 'How is it that ye have no faith?' 'Fear not, only believe.' Faith then is

closely akin to courage, a practical attitude which favours
adventure and is willing to take risks.

A 38f

A person's faith is his supreme principle of valuation. It is only
by our faith that we can decide what is most worth having in
life, among all the things that are worth having. Without a faith,
I shall find everything that attracts me in life equally valuable
and I shall be without the capacity to choose between them. I
shall be governed by my likes and dislikes; and as these shift
and change by the accidents of the changing world in which we
live, I shall be without unity of purpose, tossed about from one
accidental want to another. And the life that is without a persistent and controlling principle of order in its choices is a life
without order and without sanity. A society without a common
faith is in a like case. It is without inner unity, without the
power to choose and to stand by its choice. It will be divided
against itself; and a house divided against itself cannot stand.

Now our trouble is that we have lost our faith. There is
nothing that we clearly, supremely and continuously believe in
and are willing to stake our lives upon. And until we find a
faith to live by, life will continue to be too much for us. We shall
be at the mercy of the 'inexorable laws' that we hear so much
about. We shall be without the power of selection — like bad
wireless sets that have no selectivity and respond to every
vibration that strikes their aerials. And we shall go on pitying
ourselves and commiserating with ourselves and blaming circumstances or other nations or other people for the troubles that
are merely the reflection of our own inner lack of power to act
decisively. When I look back upon our national history during
and since the War I am forced, indeed, to the conclusion that we
richly deserve all the troubles that have come upon us, and that
so far, at least, history has let us off lightly.

This sort of thing has been said before; and we have had
plenty of exhortations to recover our faith. But we feel rightly
that it is not so simple a matter. The other side of it is equally
important, and it is this: men and women cannot believe to
order. A faith is not a thing that we can force upon ourselves or
accept ready made. It must be really credible: that is the first
thing. It must make direct and obvious contact with the circumstances of our daily life: that is the second. And the third is the
most important of all — it must draw to itself the whole current

of our emotional life, and release it in a flood of spontaneous and joyful activity. It must make us believe in life, believe in living, and believe in our own living selves. It is no use to offer us a faith that does not do these things; it is no use pretending to accept a faith that cannot unify the whole activity of our lives in just the circumstances of the modern world. And the faith we have lived by hitherto has failed us. That is why we are in a dilemma. We cannot any longer really believe in the things that our fathers lived by. If we are to recover our faith, it will have to be a faith that *we* can live by, individually and as a world of men and women. For the first thing that a faith must do for us is to make life thoroughly worth living.

FMW 25–27

– 21 –

Religion

As we would expect after reading Macmurray's attack on idealism, he roots religious belief firmly in the ordinary experiences of human life. Religion is a recognition of our personal nature. It celebrates our common life, and helps to maintain and deepen that fellowship.

In its central function, it [religion] brings to consciousness the implicit human intention of unity in fellowship — with its principles of equality and freedom. It maintains the intention in consciousness, deepens and strengthens it, and directs it towards its day to day realization in the co-operative activities of the group. As an expression of conscious reflection, it enlarges the field of fellowship in time; linking the living with their dead and with the generations unborn. In this way it creates the sense of the group as continuing through time, overcoming death and the fear of death, and laying the foundations of history ... This is the significance of ancestor-worship as a form of primitive religion ... It guides the intention of fellowship to its realization in co-operative activity, so giving rise to conscious techniques, to fertility rites and all forms of magic. In this field also it exhibits the extending and generalizing activities of reflection. It provides and enforces general techniques of relationship in the practical life which are valid for all its members, so laying the foundations of morality and law. Since the fellowship has to be realized under the conditions imposed by Nature, it provides a consciousness of Nature and the powers of Nature as objective conditions of practical fellowship, and directs the intentionality of the group towards them ... This is the significance of primitive Nature worship ... Since it is concerned with intentionality, it has to *symbolize* its objectives; consequently its primary expressions are ritual activities in which all members of the community share. These religious rituals are parts of the common life; but they have a special characteristic which separates them from the other, ordinary parts, and which gives them an extraordinary character. They have a *meaning:* they refer beyond themselves, beyond the present immediacy of common experience, to what is not present. They *represent* what is hoped for, what is feared, what is purposed in common. So, on the subjective side, primitive religion is an awareness and enjoyment of fellowship, as well as an affirmation of it; while on its objective side it is a technique for the achievement of common intentions *through representation.* Religion is thus the matrix of all the representative activities of human consciousness, and of their rationality: of their rationality, because representation, as an activity of the imagination, is necessarily private and individual, and religion is concerned with community. So it involves the demand that the private activities of the imagination should conform to the conditions of community and be valid for all. Religion, then, is the original creator of *tradition,* which is the total common awareness of the group, as a persisting community. Tradition includes, on its practical side, awareness of the rules and techniques which are valid for maintaining the common life both as co-operation and as fellowship; and on its reflective side, a mythology which is valid for all its members, an orthodoxy of common belief.

CF 86f

Primitive religion is exclusive. It is the religion of a 'kinship group,' and is limited to the 'kin.' We have already noticed the confusion of the organic relation of kinship with the personal unity of fellowship. This is natural in primitive society, for two reasons: firstly, because primitive society is as nearly organic as any human group can be, and secondly, because the natural family provides the environment within which personal relationships can most easily be established and maintained. But in the development of society the inclusion in the group of members who are not related by blood, through fusion, through inter-marriage or in any other fashion, has the effect of distinguishing between the organic and the personal unities. Men who are not related by blood behave 'like brothers.' So 'brotherhood' acquires a metaphorical meaning, by no means either sentimental or mystical, and comes to denote the state of being in fellowship, and religion becomes the expression of a consciousness of community irrespective of kinship, and borrows the terminology of kinship for a new and personal use.

When this distinction has been made, religion becomes

potentially universal. When its implications are realized in reflection, the idea of a universal religion emerges. In the fullness of time, when the social pressures demand it, universal religions are founded. They are founded by individual persons, of high religious insight, who seek a personal community denied or frustrated by the character of the societies of which they are members, and who seek to realize the potential universality of personal fellowship.

CF 90

The field of religion is the whole field of common experience organized in relation to the central fact of personal relationship. It is the personal data which are central, and form the focus of attention. Everything else is seen, from the religious point of view, in its relation to personality. The personal is the fact of central importance. All other facts are valued in relation to this central value. To put it in simpler if less exact language, the field of religion is the field of personal relations, and the datum from which religious reflection starts is the reciprocity or mutuality of these. Its problem is the problem of communion or community. Religion is about fellowship and community, which are facts of direct, universal human experience.

SRE 43

... the structure of human experience, dependent as it is for its very existence upon the mutual relations of persons, is religious in its texture. It is this primary fact about us that gives rise to religion, and since this is a universal fact about human life, belonging to its very nature, it follows that religion is an inseparable component of human life and always must be. To say that religion belongs to the early stages of human life and is destined to be superseded as human development goes on is to talk foolishness. That could only be true if progress reached the point when we were all hatched out by the sun on desert islands and lived and died without knowing that there was anyone else in the world but our solitary selves. A person who has no religion, or a society which has repudiated religion, has merely forgotten that humanity exists only in the relation of human beings to one another.

SRE 46

I submit, therefore, that the reflection of childish dreams in religion proves not that religion itself is irrational, but only that it is still immature and has not discovered its own meaning and its proper function. To this I must add that the spread of the conviction, in any community, that religion is a childish super- stition, though it is no evidence against the rationality of religion, is the strongest possible evidence that the personal rela- tions of its members are irrational and that the community is in process of dissolution. For a community consists in the structure of personal relations between its members.

SRE 58

We have seen how, in moments of stress, the bond of affection may be turned into opposition, and how the common life of co- operation may then preserve the relationship until affection is restored by forgiveness and reconciliation. In the case of society the reverse of this takes place. In times of stress, as for example when the society is threatened by attack from another society and its structure of co-operation for the supply of its needs is threatened with destruction, the society has to depend, for the preservation of its unity, upon the mutual affection of its mem- bers, that is to say, upon their emotional attachment and loyalty to one another as members of the same society. If that loyalty is not strong enough to preserve the unity until the normal working of its co-operative structure is restored, the society will perish. The more complicated the structure of co-operation in a society becomes, the more liable it is to break down. This means that it becomes more dependent upon the strength of the bonds of affection between its members. And the more extensive the society becomes the more difficult it becomes to create and sustain those bonds of common loyalty on which the possibility of effective co-operation depends. The development of society throughout history is fundamentally an increase in the number of people who become members of one society, that is to say, interdependent in co-operation for the supply of their needs. But this is possible only by the creation and maintenance of a bond of loyalty which unites an ever-increasing number of people in loyalty to one another as members of the same human brotherhood.

SRE 60f

In Macmurray's view it is the reverse of the truth to see religion as a private and individual concern, since it arises from the experience of shared life. Macmurray would have agreed with those who say that religious belief is 'a personal matter,' but he would not have identified 'personal' with 'private,' since our person-hood is fulfilled through our relationships with other persons. Private activities such as solitary prayer and meditation are part of the 'rhythm of withdrawal and return,' and their purpose is, or should be, to encourage a renewed and more effective participation in communal life.

As a result of this primary dissociation, religion becomes a private matter for the individual. It is no longer, that is to say, essentially a matter of real mutuality, but a relation of the individual in reflection to his own ideals and aspirations. Consequently, it no longer carries the intention of a return to an increasing range and intensity of common life. Religion becomes 'what an individual does with his solitariness,' to use a phrase to which Professor Whitehead has given currency. But this means that when he does return to the practical life of mutual relationship he returns to it at the non-reflective, unintentional level, and the function of religion in relation to practical mutuality is frustrated. Religion, in this way, ceases to function in relation to normal life. The same holds true of a society whose religion has become 'other-worldly.' Religion is dissociated from the mutual co-operation of the common life. The reference from one to the other is no longer recognized. The real life of the society is then a secular life, and its intentional basis is deprived of the support of the religious consciousness and becomes a mere co-operation unsupported by the intention of fellowship. In that case, any threat to its structure leaves the society unable to sustain the system of co-operation through the sense of brotherhood in adversity. Its religion has become socially ineffective and functionless.

SRE 102f

Lastly, there is a simple reason for the tendency to dissociate the reflective aspect of religion from its practical aspect, and so to turn religion into sentimentality and illusion. The achievement of satisfactory mutual relationships in real life is not merely the primary task which life sets us, it is also the hardest and the one from which we most easily recoil. Reflection reveals not merely a world of possibility but a world of fear, and of all things in the world we fear one another most. Anyone who has made the attempt to create a common life of intimate relationship with another person — and everyone who has been married has made the attempt — must know just how difficult it is, and how natural it is to give up the task and be content in practice with the achievement of a reasonably satisfactory compromise which falls far short of the intention with which the effort began. The dreams of a complete and perfect intimacy over the whole range of a life completely shared remain. But the intention to realize them in practice is weakened and disappears.

SRE 112f

Religion and unreality

Religion, therefore, has two aspects, ritual and doctrine. The first is aesthetic in form, the second scientific. Of the two aspects, the aesthetic is the positive and primary, since it is valuational, and refers to the intention of action; the scientific is secondary and negative, since the means presupposes the end. These aspects are not, of course, science and art; the distinction has reference only to their form. As aspects of religion they are held together and complement one another — looking to their integration in action. Or, to put it otherwise, both refer to the unity of action which constitutes reality; the one to its aspect as fact, the other to its aspect as value. The one refers to an absolute Truth which is the standard of all partial truths; the other to an absolute Satisfactoriness (or Goodness) which is the standard of all partial goods. In their togetherness they symbolize the unity of Truth and Goodness. But this unity is realized only in action; so that reality is symbolized as the one action which intends the unity of Truth and Goodness, and which achieves its end with absolute efficiency. To this we must add that the problem of the unreal is the problem of the personal, and action depends upon the relation of persons. The absolute intention must, therefore, be the realization of a universal community; the means to this the actuality of the world as history. This can only be satisfactorily expressed in religious terms, as we should expect; since no form of reflection can be adequately translated into another. The language of religion, which wrestles with the problematic of the personal, is necessarily a personal language. We might say — to use a form of words with which we are familiar — that the reality of the world is a personal God, who is the Creator of the world and the Father of all men. His work in history is the redemption of the world from evil and the setting up of the Kingdom of Heaven on earth.

If the motive which sustains a religion becomes negative, the religion itself must become unreal. In that case, the religion may either become aggressive — seeking to achieve community by force and achieving, at most, a pragmatic society; or it may become submissive, contemplative and idealistic, referring its reflective symbolism to another world; to a community which is expected but not intended. We must refrain from elaborating this theme, tempting though it is, in order to concentrate our attention upon a more urgent issue. We must consider the loosing of the ties which unite the two aspects of religion — the intellectual and the emotional — so that they enter upon an independent life of their own and become autonomous as science and art respectively.

PR 174f

All religion, I have said, is grappling with fear. When it is successful it convinces its adherents that there is nothing to be afraid of. Notice now that this may mean two quite different things. It may mean, in the first place, that none of the things you are afraid of will happen to you; that you will be saved from suffering and loss and unhappiness and death. That is the principle on which false religion is based. It is often called optimism. But it is not the only meaning that the doctrine can have. To say that there is nothing to be afraid of may mean that all the things that we are afraid of will happen or may happen to us, and that there is no reason to fear them even if they do. That is what real religion says. To the man who is afraid of poverty, it does not say: 'God will save you from losing your money.' It says: 'Suppose you do lose your money, what is there to be afraid of in that?' If it is the fear of suffering and death that haunts you, real religion says 'Yes, of course, you will suffer and, of course, you will die, but there is nothing to be afraid of in that.' It does not say, as all false religion and false idealism does in effect: 'Shut your eyes to things you are afraid of; pretend that everything is for the best in the best of all possible worlds; and there are ways and means of getting the divine powers on your side, so that you will be protected from the things you are afraid of. They may happen to other people, but God will see to it that they don't happen to you.' On the contrary, true religion says 'Look the facts you are afraid of in the face; see them in all their brutality and ugliness; and you will find, not that they are unreal, but that they are not to be feared.' If you ask me now, where is there a religion which has ever taken that line, which has refused to offer its adherents an escape from the reality of evil and suffering, the answer is 'The religion of Christ.' May I remind you of two sayings of his. 'Blessed are ye when men shall revile you and persecute you and say all manner of things falsely against you for my sake.' And another: 'In the world ye shall have tribulations, but be of good cheer, I have overcome the world.'

FMW 62–64

– 22 –

God

As we saw in Chapter 2, Macmurray believed that the main task of twentieth-century philosophy was to develop an adequate conception of personality. Only if this were done could the dominant philosophical trend of atheism be reversed.

... I had become suspicious of the influence of Greek philosophy upon the formulation of Christian doctrine from the earliest times — the times when a Greek convert, searching for the truth, could say 'Now I have discovered the true philosophy in the teaching of the Christians.' At the same time, in my own search for a satisfactory philosophy I found myself critical of the foundations of Greek philosophy, and so of all subsequent philosophy to date, and was reaching for a new philosophical form that would not exclude a belief in God, by making religion a matter of unjustifiable assertion.

PJ 3

Having rejected the organic metaphor as inappropriate to humans, Macmurray could not accept a pantheistic idea of God. He regarded any discussion of an impersonal God as a contradiction in terms.

We have hewn a rough way to the proper import of the question whether God exists. The proposition means that the ultimate reality of the universe is such that it can satisfy religious demands. God is therefore necessarily personal. On no other terms can the demands of the religious experience be satisfied, since the relations which are the stuff of religious life are personal relations. God must be judge, confidant and helper. Can prayer be addressed to the impersonal? Can we have fellowship with a tree or a rabbit? There can be no question of an impersonal God. The phrase is a contradiction in terms. The religious assertion of the existence of God is either the assertion that the supreme reality is personal or it is empty of any specific meaning. It may, of course, be argued that the supreme reality is not personal; but it should be clearly understood that to do so is to defend an atheistical position, and to deny that religion is objectively true, however essential to human well-being we may admit it to be. The idea of God, whether it be a real or a ficti-tious idea, is emphatically the idea of a Personality, responsible for the existence and character of the universe, constituting the ultimate reality of the world, in terms of which alone life and nature can finally be understood.

A 183f

... the conception of God at which we have arrived is not pan-theistic. Pantheism results from the attempt to give a religious colour to an organic conception of the world. A personal con-ception alone is fully theistic and fully religious. For there can be no action without an agent, and an agent, whether finite or infinite, though he is immanent in existence, necessarily trans-cends it. For the existent is what has been determined, and the agent is the determiner. What has been determined is the past; but the agent is concerned with the future and its determination. So in action he passes beyond his existence, transcending the past which constitutes his determinate being. His reality as agent lies in his continual self-transcendence. God, therefore, as the infinite Agent is immanent in the world which is his act, but transcendent of it. The terms 'transcendent' and 'immanent' refer to the nature of persons as agents, and they are strictly correla-tive. Pure immanence, like pure transcendence, is meaningless. Whatever is transcendent is necessarily immanent; and imma-nence, in turn, implies transcendence.

It would be a mistake to suppose that this vindication of the validity of religious belief in general constitutes an argument for the truth of any system of religious belief in particular. Religious doctrines are as problematic as scientific theories and require like them a constant revision and a continual verification in action. Their verification differs in this, that it cannot be experimental, since they are not merely pragmatic; they can be verified only by persons who are prepared to commit them-selves intentionally to the way of life which they prescribe.

PR 223

Macmurray saw the traditional arguments for the existence of God as misconceived, and irrelevant to his own conception of God. Nevertheless, as a scientist he was prepared to grant some credence to the 'argument from design.'

The God of the traditional proofs is not the God of religion.

One of these proofs, the argument from design, has seemed more resistant to criticism than the others. Kant, who more than any other philosopher was responsible for unearthing the logical flaw in these arguments, gave it a qualified approval. I should not wish to rest the case for religion upon it; but it may be worth while pointing out in passing that contrary to a good deal of current belief, the progress of science has enormously strengthened the argument from design. The original argument was based upon macroscopic and superficial evidences of design in Nature; and to these could be opposed similar evidences of the absence of design. But science has silenced this opposition by revealing its superficial and merely *prima facie* character. It has revealed a microscopic orderliness of structure in Nature underlying and sustaining both what looks like order and what looks like disorder on the surface. This structured order is breathtaking in its intricacy, and seems infinite in its extent. Every increase in the adequacy of our instruments of investigation serves only to reveal a further delicacy of structure in the order of nature. But science has only revealed and described this infinite orderliness with increasing adequacy. It has done nothing at all to explain it. It is a total error to think that science has provided an alternative explanation. We must conclude from this that if the argument from design in nature to the existence of God ever had any cogency — and this is indeed doubtful — the advance of science has increased its cogency a thousandfold.

If this were all, it would yield little to the point. For the existence of orderly structure, however fine, is not in itself evidence of *design*. Design implies a purposeful adaptation of means to ends. There is another aspect of the matter, however, which Kant with his usual penetration has called to our notice. It is that the order of nature is adapted to our modes of knowing and so comprehensible to us. Why should this be so? Why should the world not have been structured with infinite delicacy, but in a mode which passed our comprehension and of which we had no means even to be aware? How does it come about that at times the scientist, by purely theoretical calculation can define in advance an unknown aspect of the order of nature which is then looked for and found? And all these ways of thinking, such as mathematical calculation, have their origin, and their primary uses, in the service of our human purposes. They are devices we have elaborated as means to our ends. Is it not something of a miracle, then, that they should turn out to be means to a comprehension of the orderly structure of the world? Unless, perhaps, something like that capacity for thought which enables us to order our activities is at work in the ordering of the world? It is this, rather than the mere fact of orderliness, which is the nerve of the argument from design. It was this consideration, no doubt, that led Kant to except this argument from his condemnation of the others. Even so, and here we must follow Kant, it does not prove the existence of God, since existence cannot be proved. At the most it makes the belief in God a reasonable belief.

PR 207f

– 23 –

The meaning of Christianity

Macmurray believed the ancient Hebrews to have fully understood the nature of human life (see Chapter 18). In his view, the significance of Jesus is to have recognized what this insight implied: that the community which fulfils our personal nature cannot be restricted to one tribe, race or nation, but must be realized universally.

We must understand Jesus as the fully mature expression of the Jewish consciousness; as the final unfolding, in clear consciousness, of the implications of the Hebrew conception of the significance of social history. The main difficulty in doing this lies in the fact that our own consciousness is not religious in its structure, and that we therefore tend to interpret the teaching and the behaviour of Jesus in terms of *our* modes of thought rather than his. We have to remind ourselves that ideas and phrases change their significance if the mode of consciousness in which they are thought is changed. We tend to think about Jesus as if he were a European, and to ask questions which could only have a significance if he were. We may find ourselves asking, 'Was Jesus a social reformer?' Such a question has a specific meaning only in a dualist mode of thought. It implies a contrast and a conflict between a spiritual world and a material world, and inevitably suggests that Jesus must have been *either* concerned with social organization *or* with religion. But we have seen that the main characteristic of the Jewish religious consciousness is that this distinction does not arise. It is an integral consciousness, for which social history is the content of religious experience, and social behaviour the criterion of religious reality. Jesus, like any of the Hebrew prophets, could not make a religious assertion without making a demand upon social behaviour.

CH 43

... to say that Jesus was *both* concerned about men's spiritual life *and* about the conditions of their material life is to distinguish the two in a way that is only possible for a non-religious mind. For the religious consciousness a statement about society is a religious statement and a statement about God has an immediate and direct reference to society. This is the clue to any understanding of Jesus. He is not an idealist — for the same reason that he is not a materialist — because the distinction between the ideal and the material does not arise for him.

CH 44

Jesus was the man in whom the religious significance of the world was revealed in a definite and complete form. The definiteness and completeness mean that the religious consciousness has reached the point at which the universal significance of human history has become explicit in human consciousness. We might put this in a non-religious form by saying that Jesus discovered the significance of human life. In its religious form the assertion would be that Jesus became conscious of the intention of God in human history. Thus Jesus marks the point in history at which it becomes possible for man to adopt consciously as his own purpose the purpose which is already inherent in his own nature. The mission of Jesus to his own people is to reveal to them what has been implicit in their cultural history from the beginning, to declare to them what they are called to do and to demand their acceptance of the task and of its conditions.

CH 55

... in trying to understand the teaching of Jesus, we divide the theoretical element from the practical. This can be best realized in an example. When Jesus says, 'Blessed are the meek for they shall inherit the earth,' our tendency is to treat this as an assertion that humility is one of the supreme virtues, and we go on to point out how distinctive of the teaching of Jesus, when compared with the teaching of other moralists, is this stress upon humility as a virtue. A sermon on this text is almost inevitably a sermon on the virtue of humility. I find it difficult to imagine it as a sermon on how to inherit the earth. Indeed it is more likely to lead to a general injunction against the desire to be successful in the material field, and so to become a panegyric on those who turn from an interest in this world to a purely 'spiritual' conception of goodness. It is this kind of treatment of the teaching of Jesus that gives point to the communist contention that religion is 'opium for the people' and that it is used to persuade the poor and unfortunate classes to be content with their lot. Yet it is quite obvious that Jesus gave as his reason for believing in humility that it was an essential part of the means to ultimate material success. Nothing could be less characteristic of the mind of Jesus than the notion that virtue is its own reward.

CH 50

Where the sentiment of kinship, either real or imaginary, is the basis of unity which a religion fosters, such a religion organizes emotion and culture towards the past and sanctifies tradition and custom. It is necessarily a *reactionary* religion in a situation which calls for progress. But a religion which has rejected such a basis; which has, like Christianity, substituted the sentiment of common humanity as its basis of relationship, organizes emotion and culture *towards the future* and sanctifies the society that is to come, in which all exclusive relationships have been subordinated to the society of men and women, as men and women, in a brotherhood of mankind. Christianity is inherently a *revolutionary* religion seeking the achievement of a world community. It is *about* a new society that has to be brought into being through the transformation of existing societies. All this is implied already in the rejection by Jesus of the Jewish 'kinship' religion, and it is already explicit in the New Testament. 'In Christ Jesus,' says St Paul, 'there is neither Greek nor Jew, barbarian, Scythian, bond nor free.'

CC 42

The notion of freedom as the result of the teaching of Jesus is the key to the writings of St Paul, in which the contrast between the freedom of the Gospel and the bondage of the Law continually finds expression, and there also we find it connected with the idea of truth. He says, for example, in writing to the Christian community in Galatia, 'O foolish Galatians, who hath bewitched you that ye should not obey the truth? ... Stand fast, therefore, in the liberty wherewith Christ hath made us free and be not entangled again with the yoke of bondage.' Thus, for Paul, the hallmark of Christian community is its freedom from bondage to rules and regulations, and the true human community is the free community. So on the question of keeping

Sabbaths he says, 'One man esteemeth one day above another: another esteemeth every day alike. Let every man be fully persuaded in his own mind. He that regardeth the day, regardeth it unto the Lord; and he that regardeth not the day, to the Lord he doth not regard it.' Here the freedom of the Gospel expresses itself in the demand for individual variety in social behaviour, and against the effort to stereotype even the forms of religious observance in the community. Paul even goes to the length of asserting the principle of anarchism, 'all things are lawful unto me;' though he goes on to qualify it by adding that all things are not expedient. And his principle of expediency is in terms of the intention of community. 'If meat make my brother to offend I shall eat no flesh while the world standeth, lest I make my brother to offend.'

CH 73

In practice Christianity has failed again and again to work towards the freedom which would accompany the creation of a fully human community. It has upheld various forms of social order which are denials of such freedom, and obstacles to it.

In the first place we must agree — and even insist — that our historian is largely right. Throughout the history of Europe, the Christian religion has functioned largely as a conservative religion, and consequently as the bulwark of the privileges of the upper classes. It does so as much to-day as at any other time. And in a revolutionary situation such as the present its weight is thrown, by and large, on the side of the old community against the new. Present-day religion is clearly, on the whole, conservative religion.

CC 47

We must notice one other aspect of the process by which Christianity was made to function — so far as its official expressions were concerned — as the conservative religion of a traditional form of civilization. When Christianity accepted the function of spiritual conservatism in European civilization, it had of course to defend the cultural tradition. This involved a fusion between the Christian tradition proper, which came from Hebrew sources, and the pagan traditions of Graeco–Roman culture. Elements derived from Stoicism, from Neo-Platonism, from the Aristotelian philosophy were fused together, during the long process which shaped the Mediaeval culture into a unity, to form a conception of the world, of man's place in the world, of norms of individual and social life. This vast system of belief was so intertwined with the more strictly religious aspects of Christian doctrine and theology that they formed a single whole. In this way Christianity came to be identified with a conception of the world and of life which is largely pagan in origin and almost wholly pagan in its intellectual structure, and in consequence became the bulwark of a traditional paganism which it had set out to supersede.

The result of this has been twofold. It has tended to make Christian ritual the persistent symbol of Mediaevalism in the modern world, and to keep alive a hankering for the kind of society which characterized the Middle Ages. The archaic flavour of the forms, ceremonies and ritual of the older Churches at least makes them natural centres not merely of social conservatism but of social reaction. In the second place, it has tended to identify Christianity with a set of beliefs and theories which the development of science has made increasingly incredible. Through the whole development of science, from Copernicus to Freud, the Christian Churches have been identified with the losing battle against science in defence of Mediaeval beliefs. This has meant that millions of honest people have been put in the position of having to choose between modern science and Christianity. Yet in reality, what they so rejected or defended as Christianity was largely a system of philosophy, mainly of pagan origin, which the Mediaeval church had mistakenly sponsored.

CC 51f

But we should not be discouraged by the palpable inadequacy of the existing Christian institutions. The existing political organizations, including the various Internationals, are just as inadequate and even less likely to rise to the occasion. Christianity has in the past shown an incomparable capacity for transforming and regenerating itself in the face of just such crises; and it has, in its profession, in its history and in its underlying universality and humanity the starting-point and the standing ground for the task of recreating the inner unity of Christendom. In this critical hour of human history this is the function of the Christian Church; and we have a right to ask and to expect that the Church will undertake it.

We may go farther and assert that if the Christian Church, in any of its forms or in any new form that the need of our times may determine, will accept the task that belongs to it, and fulfil the conditions of performing it, then success is certain. A Christianity which was true to its own essence would undoubtedly be adequate to the salvation of the world in our time. The Christian Church can, if it will, create the new democratic order and achieve equality without losing freedom.

CC 60f

The Jewish rejection of Christianity was a rejection of their own reality, and brought into play, as Jesus had foreseen, the law of self-frustration. Their determination to maintain an exclusive nationalism, and to sustain their own will to power, achieved its opposite. They refused to accept the call to become, of their own intention, immanent in the world as the true community — the nucleus of the kingdom of heaven. As a result, their refusal achieved, in spite of themselves, the immanence it rejected. Thus the Hebrew culture was brought into the substance of European life in a double form. It appears as two communities, neither of which is a society in the accepted European sense, because in neither case is the unity maintained by material forces. Both the Christian Church and the Jews are religious unities, *in* the European world but not *of* it, which cannot be assimilated to the structure of European society, and which are driven, whether by their own intention or against it, towards the universalizing of the type of humanity they represent; towards the destruction of the form of human life in which they are immanent. Yet the Christian community is the result of the acceptance by Gentiles of the inner significance of the Hebrew culture, and the Jewish community is the result of its rejection by the Hebrews themselves. What the two communities have in common — a principle of human unity which transcends the unity-principle of the general society in which they are embedded — sets them in opposition to the world of which they form a part. Within that common principle they stand in dialectical opposition to one another, negating one another. Both are immanent in Europe while transcending it. The 'problem' of Christianity and the 'problem' of the Jews are thus fundamentally the same problem, and neither can be solved except in the solution of the general problem of human community.

CH 124f

Macmurray believed that one of the chief obstacles facing the Christian task is the influence of Stoicism, with its emphasis on suppressing emotion. The Hebrew origins of Christianity have been too frequently obscured. Consequently it has been for so much of its history a religion of fear rather than of faith, of conservatism rather than increased human fulfilment. Macmurray nevertheless believed that Christianity, correctly conceived, holds the key to that fulfilment and to world fellowship.

Christian theology is the product, in the first instance, of an alliance in the theoretical field of Christian experience and Stoic philosophy. It has often been asserted that Stoicism was the mediating factor between Christianity and European thought; that the Stoic philosophy was a half-way house to Christianity, and paved the way for the acceptance of Christianity. Yet the opposite is the truth. Stoicism was the means by which Christianity was corrupted in Europe and side-tracked into dualism. For Stoicism is the most extreme and uncompromising form of dualistic morality, and Christianity is the uncompromising enemy of dualism. The great Stoic Emperor, doing his duty by persecuting the Christians, is the historic symbol of the true relation between Stoicism and Christianity.

                                                                                CH 138

The solution of our dilemma is to be found, I am convinced, in Christianity and only there. But — it is *not* to be found in pseudo-Christianity. Let me put the issue from another angle. Real religion will save us from our fear, but not from the things we are afraid of. Therefore any religion, any form of Christianity which offers us protection from life, defence against the consequences of our ignorance and folly and escape from the natural demands of the conditions of our human existence is spurious. To demand security is the expression of fear, and the religion that offers us security is a false religion, a religion fear-determined and death-determined. And such a religion is the greatest destructive force known to human life. Religion, like art and science, and in a more certain and commanding sense than either, cannot be prostituted to the service of ulterior motives without being defiled. You cannot use Christianity to bolster up an unjust order of society, or to save you from the perils of truth and justice and integrity.

In closing, then, we must come back to the immediate problem of our civilization. Why can we not act greatly for the solution of our international economic problems? Why do we simply watch our social system going to pieces before our eyes? Why are we paralysed? Because we are afraid, afraid of one another, afraid of ourselves, afraid of the consequences of any decisive action. We are fear-determined, and our one demand is the fear-demand, the demand for security, for protection. Our dilemma lies in the fact that the more we try to defend ourselves the more we destroy ourselves by isolating ourselves more and more from one another. You have noticed, have you not, that our efforts to solve a confessedly international problem only seem to increase nationalism? That is because it is fear that is the motive force of our efforts to solve the problem. There is only one way in which we can escape from the dilemma, and that is by destroying the fear that is at the root of it. And I know of no force in the world which is capable of doing that except Christianity.

Some of you will ask, I think, 'Do you really mean that Christianity can save us? Are you telling us that we must go back to the old faith that has failed us?' My answer is, decidedly, 'No.' I do not think that Christianity will save us from the things we are afraid of. I think it would save us from the fear of them which paralyses us. An outbreak of Christianity would be more likely to make short work of the makeshift society we have got. It seems to me that modern religion is mostly pseudo-Christianity; and my main reason for thinking so is that it is everywhere regarded, by its friends as well as by its enemies, as a bulwark of the present social system, as a social defence-mechanism, as a stand-by in our fear-struggle to uphold a tradition, in a word, as one of the expressions of our fear of life. Europe has never been Christian, least of all in the so-called Age of Faith. I see the history of our civilization as a struggle against Christianity which has been successful in the main; or, if you will, as an effort to turn the one real religion, the religion of love and of abundant life, into a fear-religion which would minister to our desire to be secured against the forces of life. In science, I repeat, Christianity has won a partial triumph, a triumph over our thought, and has set it free. But that triumph is nugatory until it makes the conquest of our emotional life and sets that free. Real Christianity stands to-day, as it has always stood, for life against death, for spontaneity against formalism, for the spirit of adventure against the spirit of security, for faith against fear, for the living colourful multiplicity of difference against the monotony of the mechanical, whether it be the mechanization of the mind, which is dogmatism, or the mechanization of the emotions, which is conformity.

FMW 64–66

The future of the Church

There is a widespread conception of religion as the cultivation of a refined spirituality. In one form it makes mysticism central; so that religion would seem to stem from mystical experience and to culminate in it. But in commoner forms it is the view that religion is for the benefit of the worshipper; reassuring, comforting and strengthening him, and securing for him the grace and favour of God. To make the essential point as simply as possible, it is a way of talking or thinking that assumes that religion is for the sake of the worshipping community, in one sense or another.

Now if religion is this, then it stands in strong contrast with Christianity as I understand it. Christianity is not for the sake of the Christians but *for the sake of the world*. The Christian Church exists not for the spiritual benefit of its members but for the salvation of the world outside it. This is the task assigned to it by Jesus, and it is the continuance of His work after His death. In the light of this we may venture a functional definition of the Church. 'The Church,' we may say, 'is the community of the disciples of Jesus working, in co-operation with God and under the guidance of His Spirit, to establish the Kingdom of Heaven on earth.'

I do not, however, believe that this contrast of religion and Christianity is valid. It arises from the dualism of spiritual and material; and this, in turn, from isolating the spiritual from its material reference. The basic dualism is between thought and action. Now there can be thought without action, but no action without thought. The material life is the spirit in practical expression, and so in *reality*. Consequently what a man believes is expressed in his way of life. If what he professes to believe differs from this, then either he is mistaken about what he believes or he is hypocritical. The spiritual life is this without the action, which alone could make it real. It is then the spirit functioning in imagination, and it can be real only through its reference to action: apart from this it is wholly imaginary.

Religion is about action because it is concerned with the whole man. A religion which is concerned only with the 'spiritual life' is a religion which leaves action out, and in which spiritual activity has no practical reference. To define Christianity as we have just done — in practical terms — is not to *exclude* the spiritual but precisely to *include* it together with the practical reference that gives it its meaning and its reality. The point I am stressing is that for the Christian, the meaning and purpose of his religion lies outside himself and not within him. He is a person 'for others,' as Jesus was; a person dedicated to the salvation of the world. This also means, however, that he is a member of a Christian community in the world, which is itself dedicated to the salvation of the world, and which can only achieve this by exhibiting, in its own action in the world, the image of the Kingdom of Heaven.

SRR 64f

Epilogue

I am inclined to think that the worst feature of modern life is its failure to believe in beauty. For human life beauty is as important as truth — even more important — and beauty in life is the product of real feeling. The strongest condemnation of modern industrial life is not that it is cruel and materialistic and wearisome and false, but simply that it is ugly and has no sense of beauty. Moral conduct *is* beautiful conduct. If we want to make the world better, the main thing we have to do is to make it more beautiful. Nothing that is not inherently beautiful is really good. We have to recapture the sense of beauty if we are not to lose our freedom. And that we can only do by learning to feel for ourselves and to feel really. This is not a side issue. It is the heart of the problem of modern civilization. We shall never be saved by science, though we may be destroyed by it. It is to art and religion that we must look; and both of these depend on freedom of feeling. Our science is the best thing we have, but it is not good enough for the task that lies before us, because it is concerned only with the things of the mind. There are signs — small signs — of a revival of interest in and reverence for beauty amongst us. But it is a small thing yet. I for one would pin my hopes to it rather than to anything else; much rather than to a revival of trade. It is vulgarity that is the matter with us — particularly the vulgarity of our moral ideas; and vulgarity is just another name for bad feeling. The only cure for it is emotional sincerity, a refusal to like anything or do anything that we don't sincerely *feel* to be worthwhile; and with that, a refusal to be frightened out of doing what we feel to be worth doing, whoever and whatever disapproves of it.

That, then, is my philosophy of freedom, so far as the limitations of time and conditions allow me to expound it. I have no doubt that it has left many questions unanswered and many ragged ends hanging loose. But I hope that the main idea of it has somehow found its way into expression. It is in fact quite simple. Self-realization is the true moral ideal. But to realize ourselves we have to be ourselves, to make ourselves real. That means thinking and feeling really, for ourselves, and expressing our own reality in word and action. And this is freedom, and the secret of it lies in our capacity for friendship.

Freedom in the Modern World 218f

References

1 John Passmore, *A Hundred Years of Philosophy* [1957]; Penguin, Harmondsworth 1968, p.572.

2 David A.S. Fergusson, *John Macmurray in a Nutshell*, Handsel Press, Edinburgh 1992, p.21.

3 A.R.C. Duncan, *On the Nature of Persons*, Peter Lang, New York 1990, p.2.

4 B.H. Streeter, C.M. Chilcott, J. Macmurray, and A.S. Russell, *Adventure: The Faith of Science and the Science of Faith*, Macmillan, London 1927.

5 For an account of the impact of these broadcasts on one particular listener, see Robert Waller, *Be Human or Die: A Study in Ecological Humanism*, Charles Knight, London 1973, p.60f and pp.66–74.

6 *Some Makers of the Modern Spirit: a Symposium*, ed. John Macmurray, Methuen, London 1933.

7 *The Philosophy of Communism*, Faber, London 1933; *Creative Society*, SCM Press, London 1935; and contributions to *Aspects of Dialectical Materialism*, with H. Levy, R. Fox, R. Page Arnot, J.D. Bernal, and E.F. Carritt; Watts, London 1934; *Marxism*, with John Middleton Murry, N.A. Holdaway, and G.D.H. Cole; Chapman & Hall, London 1935; and *Christianity and the Social Revolution*, ed. J. Lewis, K. Polanyi, and D.K. Kitchin; Gollancz, London 1935.

8 On the Adelphi Centre, see John Carswell, *Lives and Letters*, Faber, London 1978, Chapter 15; and Rayner Heppenstall, *Four Absentees* [1960]; Cardinal, London 1988, pp.88–98.

9 The Terry Lectures at Yale University in 1936 were published as *The Structure of Religious Experience*, Faber, London 1936; and the Deems Lectures at the University of New York, also in 1936, were published as *The Boundaries of Science*, Faber, London 1939.

10 See Craig Beveridge and Ronald Turnbull, *The Eclipse of Scottish Culture*, Polygon, Edinburgh 1989, pp.96–99.

11 In 1949 Macmurray delivered the Chancellor Dunning Trust Lectures at Queen's University, Kingston, Ontario, which were published as *Conditions of Freedom*, Faber, London 1950.

12 See Willa Muir, *Belonging*, Hogarth Press, London 1968, pp.262, 264f, 278; Vi Hughes, 'Scottish college to fight its own battle,' *Times Higher Education Supplement* (29/9/95).

13 Stuart Hampshire's *Thought and Action*, Chatto & Windus, London 1959, and Anthony Kenny's *Action, Emotion and Will*, RKP, London 1963, deal with subjects on which Macmurray had written at length, but do not refer to him.

14 *The Self as Agent*, Faber, London 1957, p.15.

15 A transcript of the programme was published in *Quaker Monthly*, Vol. 45 No.4, April 1966. The psychiatrist may possibly have been Dr Anthony Storr, who reviewed Macmurray's Gifford Lectures in the *Times Literary Supplement.*

16 For a fuller account of this topic see Philip Conford, 'Psychological Influence,' *Times Higher Education Supplement* (8/8/86).

17 John Shotter, *Images of Man in Psychological Research,* Methuen, London 1975.

18 Fergusson, *op. cit.,* p.21.

19 *Persons in Relation,* Faber, London 1961, p.224.

20 A.J. Ayer, *Language, Truth and Logic,* Gollancz, London 1936.

21 *Quaker Monthly,* Vol. 45 No. 4, April 1966, p.51.

22 Emmanuel Mounier, *Personalism,* Routledge, London 1952, p.viii.

23 J.B. Coates, *The Crisis of the Human Person,* Longmans Green, London 1949, p.9.

24 Emmanuel Mounier, *Be Not Afraid,* Rockliff, London 1951, p.113.

25 *Ibid.,* p.176.

26 *Ibid.,* pp.149f.

27 For a detailed analysis of similarities between the ideas of Macmurray and those of Mounier, readers are referred to my essay 'John Macmurray and Emmanuel Mounier: Personalist Parallels,' in the forthcoming Humanities Press symposium edited by Harry A. Carson.

28 For Mounier's reference to Macmurray, see *Personalism,* Routledge, London, 1952, p.*xx.* An account of Mounier's address to the London Personalist Group is given in Leslie Paul's foreword to Mounier's *Be Not Afraid,* Rockliff, London 1951, p.*x.* Macmurray's foreword appeared in J.B. Coates, *A Common Faith or Synthesis,* Allen & Unwin, London 1942.

29 *The Self as Agent,* Faber, London 1957, p.98.

30 Martin Pawley, *The Private Future: Causes and Consequences of Community Collapse in the West,* Thames & Hudson, London 1973, pp.12f.

31 David Smail, *The Origins of Unhappiness,* HarperCollins, London, 1993.

32 Compare Emmanuel Mounier, *Personalism,* Routledge, London 1952, pp.18f.

33 Quoted in Gerard Kelly, 'Off-the-self [*sic*] sociology,' *Times Higher Education Supplement* (24/3/95).

34 Smail, *op. cit.,* p.92.

35 *The Guardian* (6/10/95).

36 Shirley Robin Letwin, *The Anatomy of Thatcherism,* HarperCollins, London 1992, p.344.

37 *Quaker Monthly,* Vol. 45 No. 4, April 1966, p.49.

Select bibliography and further reading

Books by John Macmurray:

Freedom in the Modern World, Faber, London 1932; Humanities Press, New Jersey, USA 1991.

Interpreting the Universe, Faber, London 1933; Humanities Press, New Jersey, USA 1993.

The Philosophy of Communism, Faber, London 1933.

Reason and Emotion, Faber, London, 1935; new ed. 1995.

Creative Society: a Study of the Relation of Christianity to Communism, SCM Press, London 1935.

The Structure of Religious Experience, Faber, London 1936.

The Clue to History, SCM Press, London 1938.

The Boundaries of Science: a Study in the Philosophy of Psychology, Faber, London 1939.

Challenge to the Churches: Religion and Democracy, Kegan Paul, London 1941.

Constructive Democracy, Faber, London 1943.

Conditions of Freedom, Faber, London 1950; Humanities Press, New Jersey, USA 1993.

The Form of the Personal, (being the Gifford Lectures given in the University of Glasgow 1953–54): Vol.1 *The Self as Agent*, Faber, London 1957, new ed. 1995; Vol.2 *Persons in Relation*, Faber, London 1961, new ed. 1995.

Religion, Art and Science: a Study of the Reflective Activities in Man, Liverpool University Press, 1961.

Search for Reality in Religion, Allen & Unwin, London 1965; Quaker Home Service, London 1984.

John Macmurray also contributed to the following books:

Adventure: The Faith of Science and the Science of Faith, B.H. Streeter, C.M. Chilcott, J. Macmurray and A.S. Russell, Macmillan, London 1927.

Some Makers of the Modern Spirit: a Symposium, ed. J. Macmurray, Methuen, London 1933.

Aspects of Dialectical Materialism, H. Levy, J. Macmurray, R. Fox, R. Page Arnot, J.D. Bernal and E.F. Carritt, Watts & Co., London 1934.

Marxism, J. Middleton Murry, J. Macmurray, N.A. Holdaway and G.D.H. Cole, Chapman & Hall, London 1935.

Christianity and the Social Revolution, ed. J. Lewis, K. Polanyi and D.K. Kitchin, Gollancz, London 1935.

Freedom: its Meaning, ed. R. Anshen, Allen & Unwin, London 1942.

This Changing World, ed. J.R.M. Brumwell, Routledge, London 1944.

Quakers Talk to Sixth Formers, ed. H. Loukes, Friends Home Service Committee, London 1970.

The Personal Universe, ed. T. Wren, Humanities Press, Atlantic Highlands, New Jersey, 1975.

John Macmurray also wrote the following pamphlets:

Christianity and Communism, with Professor H. G. Wood, Industrial Christian Fellowship, London 1934.

A Philosopher Looks at Psychotherapy, C.W. Daniel, London 1938.

Foundations of Economic Reconstruction, National Peace Council, London 1943.

Idealism against Religion, Lindsey Press, London 1944.

To Save from Fear, Friends Home Service Committee, London 1964.

The Philosophy of Jesus, Friends Home Service Committee, London 1973.

The following works provide a general introduction to the philosophy of John Macmurray:

D.A.S. Fergusson, *John Macmurray in a Nutshell,* Handsel Press, Edinburgh 1992.

J. Warren, *Becoming Real: an Introduction to the Thought of John Macmurray,* Ebor Press, York 1989.

More detailed, and more philosophically demanding, is A.R.C. Duncan's *On the Nature of Persons,* Peter Lang, New York, 1990.

Macmurray's philosophy forms the basis of Frank G. Kirkpatrick's *Community: a Trinity of Models,* Georgetown University Press, Washington D.C. 1986.

Two very different journals have in recent years focused on the work of Macmurray:

The Summer 1993 edition (No. 73) of *Chapman* — 'Scotland's Quality Literary Magazine,' as it styles itself — contained articles on Macmurray by Robert Calder, A.R.C. Duncan and Stanley M. Harrison.

Harrison was guest editor of Vol. VI, No. 4 (Summer 1992) of *Philosophy and Theology* (produced by Marquette University, Wisconsin), which was devoted to Macmurray's ideas.

An international symposium on a wide variety of aspects of Macmurray's philosophy, edited by Harry A. Carson, is currently in preparation for Humanities Press, New Jersey, USA.

Appendix

Organizations promoting the thought of John Macmurray

The John Macmurray Society was founded in Canada in 1971 with John Macmurray's blessing, thanks to the initiative of the late T. Reginald Sayers. Under the laws of Ontario it was granted a Charter in the mid-1970s as a non-profit, educational association. The Society has undertaken a great deal of bibliographical research, and has reprinted a number of out-of-print writings by Macmurray; the Society also organizes conferences and lectures. The Society's current President is Father Jack Costello, S.J., who has built up a comprehensive collection of Macmurray's writings at Regis College, part of the University of Toronto's School of Theology. Father Costello can be contacted at: Regis College, 15 St Mary Street, Toronto, Ontario, Canada M4Y 2R5.

In Britain, the John Macmurray Fellowship was founded in 1993 'with the aim of advancing public knowledge of the work of John Macmurray and of promoting the teaching and development of his work.' The Fellowship issues a Newsletter and holds an annual conference with international speakers. It is currently involved in establishing links with the Personalist Forum, an international group of scholars which is planning a Centre for Personalist Studies at Westminster College, Oxford. The Chairman of the Fellowship is Philip Hunt, who can be contacted at: 93 Station Road, Llanishen, Cardiff CF4 5UU.